Financial Management
of Life Insurance Companies

Huebner International Series on Risk, Insurance, and Economic Security

J. David Cummins, Editor
The Wharton School
University of Pennsylvania
Philadelphia, Pennsylvania, USA

Series Advisors:
Dr. Phelim P. Boyle, University of Waterloo, Canada
Dr. Jean Lemaire, University of Pennsylvania, USA
Professor Akihiko Tsuboi, Kagawa University, Japan
Dr. Richard Zeckhauser, Harvard University, USA

Financial Management
of Life Insurance Companies

edited by

J. David Cummins
The Wharton School
University of Pennsylvania

Joan Lamm-Tennant
Villanova University

Kluwer Academic Publishers
Boston / Dordrecht / London

Distributors for North America:
Kluwer Academic Publishers
101 Philip Drive
Assinippi Park
Norwell, Massachusetts 02061 USA

Distributors for all other countries:
Kluwer Academic Publishers Group
Distribution Centre
Post Office Box 322
3300 AH Dordrecht, THE NETHERLANDS

Library of Congress Cataloging-in-Publication Data

Financial management of life insurance companies / edited by J. David
   Cummins, Joan Lamm-Tennant.
                p.   cm. -- (Huebner international series on risk, insurance
   and economic security)
      Papers prepared for the Symposium on Life Insurance Company
   Financial Management, held at the Wharton School in Nov. 1992.
      Includes bibliographical references.
      ISBN 0-7923-9354-6 (acid-free paper)
      1. Insurance, Life--Finance--Congresses. 2. Insurance, Life--
   Investments--Congresses. 3. Insurance, Life--Management--Congresses. I.
   Cummins, J. David. II. Lamm-Tennant, Joan. III. Series
   HG8844.F56   1993
   368.3'2'00681--dc20
                                                                    93-19221
                                                                    CIP

Printed on acid-free paper.

Printed in the United States of America

Contents

Foreword

This book is published to commemorate the 50th Anniversary of the S.S. Huebner Foundation for Insurance Education. Administered at the Wharton School of the University of Pennsylvania, the Huebner Foundation was established in 1941 to strengthen insurance education at the collegiate level by increasing the number of professors specializing in insurance and enriching the literature in the field. The financial support of leading life insurance companies has enabled the Foundation to provide post-graduate education for prospective insurance teachers and scholars. Through its fellowship program, the Foundation supports students in the Ph.D. program in Risk and Insurance at the Wharton School.

The success of the Foundation is measured by the accomplishments of its alumni. Former Huebner Fellows play leading roles in every major area of insurance education. Fellows teach insurance to tens of thousands of undergraduate and MBA students each year and have written hundreds of books and thousands of articles on insurance. Fellows hold leadership positions at the American College, the Life Office Management Association, and the Certified Employee Benefit Specialist Program.

The Foundation was created in honor of Dr. Solomon S. Huebner, a pioneer in insurance education. Dr. Huebner taught the first organized course on the economics of insurance ever offered at the collegiate level in 1904. An internationally recognized author and teacher, Dr. Huebner had a profound impact on both insurance education and the insurance industry. He served on the faculty of the Wharton School for more than nearly fifty years.

The papers in this book were prepared for the Symposium on Life Insurance Company Financial Management, held at the Wharton School in November of 1992. The Symposium was the primary event sponsored by the Foundation in celebration of its 50th Anniversary.

Attendance at the Symposium consisted of life insurance company executives and academic experts on insurance and finance.

The theme of this book is financial management, i.e., management of life insurers using techniques drawn from the field of finance. The importance of financial management has increased greatly in recent years, paralleling the growth in competition within the financial services industry. This competitive environment reflects an increasing financial sophistication among insurance consumers as well as the blurring of the lines that traditionally separated different types of financial institutions. To succeed in today's business environment, insurers must use financial techniques such as asset-liability management, financial hedging, futures, and options. They also must be increasingly precise in measuring the tradeoffs between risk and return in both their asset and product portfolios. These issues are the subject of this book.

We are grateful to Richard Phillips for his diligent efforts in preparing the final manuscript of this book and to Connie Marino for her administrative assistance.

J. David Cummins
Joan Lamm-Tennant

The Huebner Foundation gratefully acknowledges the support of EDS in sponsoring the Symposium on Life Insurance Company Financial Management and this publication.

TECHNOLOGY AND THE GLOBAL INSURANCE MARKET

Benjamin Sims
President, Commercial Insurance
EDS

EDS is pleased to have the opportunity to participate with the S.S. Huebner Foundation and the Wharton School in the Symposium on the Financial Management of Life Insurance Companies and the publication of this book.

EDS is a technology company involved, as are most life insurers, in the global insurance market. And while technology and the global insurance marketplace are each inherently interesting, there is an important trend which links them - *getting back to basics*. This trend has important implications for our personal lives and our business well-being.

In this context, I will first define this trend and then look at some examples of this trend in the personal and professional lives we all lead. Lastly, I will focus on what getting back to the basics may mean for us in the insurance industry.

The concept of getting "back to the basics" is much more than just a faddish attempt to immerse ourselves in nostalgia. "Back to the Basics" is a trend that aims to make changes in our lives and businesses that are fundamental, long-lasting and *welcome*.

A "back to the basics" approach represents a departure from instant gratification and quick fixes. Instead, it involves perseverance, continuous improvement and results achieved through tried-and-true solutions. But it's an absolutely essential trend if we are to compete successfully here and throughout the world.

How is the back to the basics trend affecting our personal lives? Let's look at some examples in the areas of education and lifestyles.

In education, the fundamentals - reading, 'riting, and 'rithmatic - are back in vogue. One of the interesting asides about the 3 R's is that there is no debate on the necessity of providing a firm educational grounding in these core areas. However, there *is* debate on implementing the changes required to get back to the basics. That debate is taking shape in communities across the nation. Whatever the outcome of those discussions, some curriculum change is inevitable if we are to ensure that the education of our youngsters is grounded in the basics.

Much to our credit, American business is playing a major role in implementing the back to the basics solution. On the local front, business has always played an important educational role. Programs like junior achievement are an ideal blending of business know-how and schooling for budding entrepreneurs.

And what better example of supporting educational initiatives is there than the support provided by insurance companies for the S.S. Huebner Foundation? The American College of Life Underwriters is another excellent example of how the insurance industry is supporting educational initiatives.

Many of our companies are also developing partnerships with schools through "Adopt-A-School" and other tutoring programs. And many of us underwrite the costs associated with developing far-reaching educational programming, delivered through a variety of media.

At EDS on the local level, we are partners with 35 elementary and middle schools from New York to California and Michigan to Texas. On the national front, we, along with Turner Broadcasting, provide systems integration and communications services for the Jason Project. This began as the dream of Dr. Robert Ballard, of the Woods Hole Oceanographic Institute, and has resulted in over a half million U.S. students participating in the discovery of the wrecks of the R.M.S. Titanic and Bismarck.

Sponsorship of programs like these needs to continue. To ensure our viability in the marketplace, we have had to step to the fore to promote the educational values that will keep our children and our businesses competitive. It's a trend that we must continue. The important thing for American business is to stay involved and play an active role with educators in rebuilding the American educational system.

Our lifestyles have also been influenced heavily by the back to the basics trend. Although the 1980s have sometimes been termed a decade of excess, in these years we also came to better appreciate the non-material aspects of our lives. In this regard, business leaders are now considering initiatives which address a variety of employee quality of life concerns. The emergence of these concerns demonstrates that we are all going through a tremendous refocusing or rebalancing of our personal and professional priorities. Issues like parental leave, paternity benefits, health care continuation and other immediate family needs are at the forefront.

But what does getting "back to basics" mean for us in the insurance industry? It means strategic financial management, the focus of the Huebner Foundation's symposium and of this book. In this context, a variety of viewpoints, advice and general observations have been offered from industry and academic leaders.

The insurance industry is refocusing itself, much the same way as the educational system, our lifestyles, and, on a more grand scale, the American economy. We have the chance before us to redefine our purpose, to recommit ourselves to the industry and to get back to the basics.

Industry chief executives suggest that just such a trend is underway. Insurance companies will need to focus on their product offerings, premium rates and a host of other issues that define them in the marketplace. But companies will also need to focus on their infrastructure - their people, work processes and technical environment - to ensure a competitive service edge. All of these elements comprise the basics of the insurance industry.

The 1980s were years of incredible product innovation. For the 1990s and beyond, the key will be determining what's basic to the success of your business. Is it junk bond or real estate investment portfolios, or is it the selling of a valued product, priced at a fair rate, and supported with superior service effort? We will no doubt encounter new and formidable challenges in the coming years.

The companies that create an environment which allows a return to the basics will be staffed by intelligent, articulate and market wise employees. The source of these individuals is our educational system. Quite simply, our business success is *directly linked* to that of our educational system. Hence, we need to continue to take the long view - both in terms of education and our business. And continue to work together to ensure our mutual success.

Financial Management
of Life Insurance Companies

1 LIFE INSURANCE AND THE QUESTION OF SOLVENCY

Salvatore R. Curiale

Superintendent of Insurance
New York State Insurance Department

I am not sure there are any serious issues confronting the life insurance industry these days, unless of course you consider solvency, liquidity, junk bonds, deteriorating mortgage and real estate portfolios, risk-based capital requirements, asset mix, separate accounts, credit risk, Congressional inquiries, shrinking surplus, demutualization and more.

What happened? How did a boring, straight-forward business become so interesting and so difficult to regulate? During the past decade the life insurance industry has undergone dramatic changes. A business that was previously characterized by stable risks and generous profits has been transformed into one marked by instability of risk and evaporating profit margins.

The change was precipitated by the dramatic rise in interest rates in the late 1970s and early 1980s. The relatively high rates offered by money market funds, Certificates of Deposit and other similar products prompted insurers to develop insurance alternatives that shifted the marketing emphasis from security to, at least partially, rate of return.

Profit margins began their descent in this environment. In many firms, marketing considerations became the driving force behind the quoted rate of return, thus indirectly influencing a company's investment decisions. Prior to this time, a company's investment philosophy would dictate the types of products the firm would sell in the marketplace.

Moreover, the matching of asset and liability cash flows took on greater significance and required an ongoing dialogue among actuarial, marketing and investment staff, a dialogue that had not previously been part of the functionally autonomous management structures that had dominated the life insurance industry for years.

As profits dwindled in the 1980s, life insurers responded in various ways. Some viewed the double-digit yields of the junk bond market as an opportunity to increase market share. A junk-dominated portfolio, they reasoned, could significantly boost yields on the annuities, guaranteed interest contracts (GICs) and life insurance products they marketed. Others devoted sizable portions of their assets to real estate investments and mortgage loans, many of which were of questionable value.

Some life insurers marketed new products whose guaranteed rates of return would come back to haunt them when interest rates plummeted, others tightened their belts and trimmed expenses. Still others sought "creative" accounting approaches as a short-term means of alleviating financial strain.

Many of the underlying problems of the life industry failed to surface during much of the eighties. Boom times are very forgiving. Anyone can appear a genius, at least temporarily. However by the latter part of the decade, a devastating confluence of negative events had begun to touch the life insurance industry. Most notably: the Savings & Loan debacle, the collapse of the junk bond market, the weakness of commercial banks, the collapse of the commercial real estate market and the burgeoning federal deficit.

Remarkably, these events had a minimal impact on the life insurance industry until the seizure by regulators of two Executive Life companies in the spring of 1991. A public that had long associated life insurers with safety and conservatism was suddenly dismayed by talk of rehabilitation, guaranty funds and reduced payments to contractholders. Pensioners who depended on Executive Life of California for their monthly allotments were particularly frightened and outraged -- frightened because their payments were suddenly in jeopardy and outraged because their employers had been permitted by the federal government to sell their pension plans to the highest bidder, pocketing any excess funds for themselves. Thousands of retired American workers felt abused, battered and confused by a system so seemingly oblivious to their needs.

At the time of the Executive Life takeovers, many viewed the action as an aberration. Executive Life's demise, they argued, was due to a few high flyers whose ravenous appetite for junk could not be satiated. Such a view was far less supportable once the Mutual Benefit Life Insurance Company was taken over by the New Jersey Insurance Department a few months later. Although Mutual Benefit had ventured into many questionable real estate and mortgage investments, it was still considered an "old guard," conservative company.

A crisis of confidence spread throughout the life insurance industry following the Mutual Benefit announcement. A sizable number of life insurers -- some with household names -- were being downgraded by the rating agencies. As a result, many life insurers with less-than-stellar ratings fell victim to a "flight to quality," a condition that invariably arises within destabilized segments of this country's financial services sector. Every insurer felt the impact of this phenomenon, especially those with large blocks of business that were in a position to walk at a moment's notice.

Today life insurers are operating on thinner surpluses. Some remain strong; others are very much in need of capital. The industry is under a microscope -- more rating agencies are making more evaluations about more life insurers than ever before. Notwithstanding such large-scale public scrutiny, policyholders and insurance consumers are clearly worried and concerned about the long-term prospects for the industry, and more specifically, the insurers that underwrite their policies.

What the Industry Can Do

The life insurance industry must establish sufficient liquidity to meet its contingencies -- the current climate requires it. In the long run, however, a highly liquid industry does not bode well for this nation's economy. This country cannot afford to lose the life insurance industry as a long-term investor. Thus, an industry-wide liquidity pool -- able to pump money into the system when needed -- is an idea worthy of serious study.

The industry must strive to improve its balance sheet in legitimate ways. Financial reinsurance -- which provides "window dressing" for the financial statement of the ceding company, while transferring no real risks -- must not be permitted. Other schemes to enhance surplus -- such as sale and leaseback arrangements and the securitization of future revenues -- are contrary to statutory accounting principles and, like financial reinsurance, cannot be tolerated.

Life companies have begun to merge in order to cut costs, expand market share and take advantage of economies of scale. Such consolidations undoubtedly will continue and should prove healthy for the industry. In addition, most life insurers are likely to focus on the types of business they do best. They can no longer be all things to all people. Once they have identified their market niches, they should be working long and hard to produce the best products.

In addition to solid products, the industry must redefine prudence with respect to its investments, linking assets and liabilities as closely as possible. It's really about getting back to basics, and perhaps that's what the 1990s will be all about, not only in insurance, but in banking, the automobile industry, retail sales and just about every other sector of the American economy.

The Regulator's Role

Public confidence in the life insurance industry must be restored. Regulators must deal quickly and successfully with companies, such as Executive Life, that are placed in Rehabilitation. I am confident that in New York, policyholders and annuitants will be made whole *without* resorting to guaranty fund assistance.

Life insurers are operating in a dynamic economic environment. Those sleepy little companies that dutifully collected premiums and paid death benefits have disappeared from the economic landscape. Under such conditions, pressures on regulators to stray from the inherent conservatism of statutory accounting can be enormous. We must, however, resist. We cannot allow gimmicks to mask an insurer's true financial condition. We cannot permit credit for reinsurance that fails to transfer risk. We cannot allow cosmetic, reversible transactions within a holding company structure designed to artificially inflate surplus.

From a product standpoint, regulators must be vigilant in ensuring that insurance policies provide real benefits and value in a competitive marketplace. We must ensure that consumers can understand the risks associated with competing products. And we must make sure that the agents and brokers we license to sell such products are providing meaningful cost comparisons and evaluations.

Conclusion

The life insurance industry is solid and solvent, yet undeniably under stress. Although this may sound like a contradiction, I do not believe it is. It's an industry that warrants the public's trust.

Confidence in the industry must be rebuilt for the sake of the public and for the sake of this country's economy. Restoring the industry's credibility among consumers is no easy task. There are no short cuts, no miracle cures. I am convinced, however, that a robust and self-sustaining life insurance industry that recognizes and responds to its own shortcomings can provide the underpinnings for a resurgence of confidence in this key sector of our economy.

2 CONSIDERATIONS IN A MUTUAL LIFE INSURANCE COMPANY CONVERSION

Harry D. Garber
Vice Chairman
The Equitable Life Assurance Society
of the United States

This chapter focuses on the issues involved in a conversion of a life insurance company from mutual to stock form. This is a subject to which I have given a great deal of thought and attention in recent years, including service as Chairman of the Society of Actuaries Task Force on Mutual Life Insurance Company Conversions and as a member of the LICONY (Life Insurance Council of New York) group that helped to design New York State's demutualization law. I am particularly pleased to see this work bear fruit for my own company which successfully implemented mutual-to-stock conversion during 1992.

Life Insurance Industry Stock-Mutual Composition

The life insurance industry is now composed of over 2,000 stock companies and about 125 mutual companies. The stock companies have about 50 percent of the assets of the industry and about 2/3 of the capital resources, and these percentages are increasing because the stock companies are growing faster than the mutuals.

Most of the present-day, large mutual companies began operations in the mid-1800's, some as stock companies and some as mutuals. For various reasons including fallout from the Armstrong investigation in New York State, there was a wave of mutualizations that took place in the first two decades of this century. By the 1920's, the current line up of companies was established and it has remained essentially the same for the last seventy-five years. There have been no major mutualizations and only a handful of demutualizations, all in the last few years.

Ownership and Financing of Mutual Insurers

The most prominent feature of a mutual company is that there are no shareholders. Rather, there are policyholders, called members, who possess some attributes of ownership. For example, members have the right to vote for directors and to receive proceeds in liquidation, but the current financial interest of individual members is not determined. There is just an undivided whole. Policyholders are also entitled to receive policy dividends which is primarily a customer (rather than an owner) interest. The management of a mutual company has an obligation to act in the interests of the company's members. For this purpose, the term "members" is not narrowly defined; it includes current and future policyholders.

From a financial perspective, the key impediment to mutual life company stability, growth and development, is that equity capital can be raised only through retained earnings from the company's operations, primarily insurance and investment. In comparison, stock companies can raise equity capital from retained earnings and from the capital markets through sales of common stock, preferred stock, debt (at the holding company level), etc. If a mutual wishes (and is able, competitively,) to raise the level of earnings retained each year, its capital is increased only by the amount of additional earnings actually retained. For a stock company, improved earnings will increase market value by a multiple of the annual improvement, with comparable effects on equity capital raising potential. Borrowing and sales of interests in subsidiary companies are often cited as ways for mutuals to raise capital, but borrowing is not a source of equity capital for mutuals, and the sale of an interest in a subsidiary -- for both mutuals and stocks -- is simply a redeployment of, and not a growth in, capital.

The cost of capital for stock life insurance companies is

determined in the same manner as for public enterprises, taking into account the market return rates on equity and debt and the applicable debt-equity ratios. For mutual companies, on the other hand, the cost of capital is effectively the percentage growth rate in capital required in order to achieve/retain the desired capital/liability ratios. For example, if the mutual company wishes to retain a 6 percent ratio of capital to liabilities and liabilities are growing at 8 percent per year, the cost of capital is 8 percent. If it wishes to grow the capital/liabilities ratio above the 6 percent level, the cost of capital would be greater than 8 percent; if the 6 percent ratio is more than the company believes is needed, the cost of capital could be lower than 8 percent. As a matter of interest, stock companies typically have higher average capital/liability ratios (10 percent) than mutual companies (6 percent). Traditionally, this difference reflected the greater risk of stock company fixed price products. It is not entirely clear why this difference in capital ratios persists today when stock and mutual companies offer essentially similar products.

Mutual - Stock Conversions: Theory and Practice

As mentioned earlier, there were virtually no mutual-to-stock life company conversions for several decades after 1920. State laws more often than not prohibited such conversions (in response to some "bad cases" that occurred in the early 1900's) and there was little desire by mutual companies to lobby for enabling legislation.[1] In the 1980's, there was a renewed interest in mutual-to-stock life company conversions. Conversions of mutual savings banks and savings and loan associations awakened interest in the life insurance industry. Increased competitiveness, higher investment market volatility and risk, and increased diversification raised capital needs of mutual life companies; these capital pressures have been compounded more recently by pressures from rating agencies, from regulators (in the form of risk-based capital standards), the general public's lowered perception of the safety of the industry, and by insurance agents reacting to these events. Given these events, a number of states have adopted enabling legislation, with the New York legislation being the most comprehensive. Although few demutualizations have occurred (e.g., UNUM, Northwestern National and Macabees, with Equitable), I believe that there is a momentum in that

---

[1] FIC article, pages 35-39.

direction and that as the benefits become apparent, others will follow.

As for the theory of conversion itself, I believe there are two key concepts. The first is the need to have a conversion plan that satisfies the requirements of all interested parties: the policyholders, the investors, and the company itself. Policyholders are entitled to fair compensation in return for giving up their membership rights, and to protection of their policy rights, including policy dividends. If policyholders do not believe they are being treated fairly in the conversion plan, they will not vote in favor of it. Investors are in a similar situation. If they believe that the anticipated result of investment in the converting company will not meet their return on investment objectives, they will simply pursue alternative investments. In addition to obtaining additional corporate flexibility from a conversion, the company itself must view the conversion process as providing additional capital on reasonable terms. The company will be seeking a successful offering, and will not proceed if it does not believe this will happen.[2]

My second point is that conversion is a market transaction -- not an allocation of book values. Many conversion statutes specify that policyholders are to receive, in the aggregate, compensation equal to the company's statutory surplus. (In the case of UNUM, this was interpreted to mean the amount of the company's pre-conversion GAAP capital.) It should be obvious that, if the aggregate amount of consideration to policyholders exceeds the value of the company, shareholders may be reluctant to invest in the company, causing the demutualization to fail. Also, in a demutualization in which the company remains independent, most of the policyholders will be given shares (of the converted company) rather than cash. It is important that the conversion plan promote the market value of the shares to assure that policyholders receive full value for their membership interest. It should be obvious from these examples, that both the demutualization plan and the enabling statute must recognize the key part the market plays in a mutual-to-stock conversion.[3]

A mutual-to-stock company conversion is effected through a plan of conversion that is adopted by the company, approved by the regulatory authorities after a hearing, and finally, approved by

---

[2] SOA report, pages 299-301.

[3] SOA Report, pages 308-313 and 314-316.

policyholder vote. The primary elements of such a plan are as follows:[4]

- *The value to be distributed to policyholders.* This encompasses (i) the total amount to be allocated to policyholders and the basis of allocation to each policyholder (which will typically reflect a fixed element as compensation for the surrender of membership rights plus a variable element based on past and expected future contributions to company values; (ii) the form of each distribution, such as shares in the newly-formed company, cash, or other benefits; and (iii) a definition of which policyholders are eligible to receive a distribution (e.g., only those currently in force).

- *The method to protect policyholder dividend interest.* A closed branch is becoming the generally accepted way of providing this protection. As defined in New York law, the converting company allocates to the closed branch sufficient assets so that the principle of and income on those assets plus the premiums and other policy income will be sufficient to pay the guaranteed benefits on existing participating contracts plus the dividends on the then current scale -- if current experience continues. The closed branch thus serves to assure that policyholders do not have to choose between conversion compensation and their policyholder dividends and benefits. The closed branch approach has been used by UNUM; it is a requirement under New York law, and it is the approach recommended by the Society of Actuaries Task Force.[5] Admittedly, however, what is great in theory often proves difficult in practice, given the need for asset valuations, expense allocations, and numerous other related tasks involved in the initial construction of the

---

[4] New York Insurance Laws, Section 7312, subsection (e); FIC Article, pages 67-69.

[5] SOA Report, pages 303-306; New York Insurance Laws, Section 7312, subsection (d)(5).

closed branch.

- *The amount of capital to be raised at conversion and whether it is to be raised privately, publicly, or through some combination of these approaches.* This issue will be discussed later.

- *The selected corporate structure.* For example, a company may choose to establish an upstream holding company and, in the process, reorganize its relationship with its subsidiaries by making them direct subsidiaries of the holding company. This would provide relief from certain regulatory requirements.

- *An ongoing operations plan.* Thought must be given to appropriate capital levels, whether to continue to issue participating products, financial projections, etc.

- *Management incentives.* This would include stock option plans, etc., and must be sensitive to any federal and state law requirements.

- *Procedural considerations.* These include policyholder voting procedures, hearing dates, form and content of materials to be mailed out -- a major project in and of itself.

- *Statement of purpose of conversion.* Of importance here is a determination that the conversion plan and the process is fair and equitable to policyholders.

It should be obvious at this point, even without touching upon the myriad of more specific elements, that a conversion plan is complex and detailed, and requires much time and effort to assemble and to discuss with regulators. But these are only the aspects of the plan that concern policyholders and regulators. We also need to consider how the plan relates to the concurrent capital-raising process.

The purposes of capital-raising at the time of a demutualization are many and varied (e.g., to provide additional equity capital; to provide cash to buy out small shareholders; to permit the establishment of a market for a company's shares -- a market in which policyholders realize their value). The company itself is responsible for success in developing this market. A story line is critical -- telling investors why they should choose to invest -- particularly if interest earnings are low and/or there appear to be greater risks from, for example, greater concentrations of real estate and junk bonds, etc.

A GAAP accounting structure must be established. This can involve a long lead-time if the company is new to GAAP accounting. If there are inactive lines that involve ongoing losses, the company must decide whether to treat them as discontinued businesses and to reserve for future losses.

Additionally, the company must develop an offering document that will be approved by the SEC and that will not damage the efforts of the company to sell its stock. To summarize, the company, and its investment bankers, must develop a plan for the marketing of its stock and execute that plan well. A key focus is the management of the after-market to assure that sales of policyholder stock shortly after the effective date do not depress the price of the stock.

Perhaps most exemplary of the interrelationship between the conversion plan and capital raising efforts is the conflict between closed branch funding and the ability of the company to attract outside investors. As the quantity of high quality investments allocated to the closed branch increases, the value of the company to outside investor may be reduced. Regulators may tend to favor such allocations, giving somewhat less importance to the stock value and its impact on the ongoing company viability and success.

A mutual life company will face a number of profound converts as it changes to a shareholder-owned enterprise. The first is the change from a private company to a public company. The company must now perform for shareholders as well as for policyholders. It must deal more with the press and with analysts -- a significant cultural change. There has to become a clear, single focus on achieving value for shareholders, versus the multiple areas of focus as a mutual. There is an increase in the cost of capital with its effects on focus, product and market decisions, etc.. Paradoxically, the company will become more open with the outside world, and less open inside.

The Future of Mutuals

In attempting to predict whether conversions of life insurance companies from mutual-to-stock form are likely to increase in the future and, eventually, to consume all mutual life companies, one needs to consider a number of factors. The first is that conversion is a long, costly and difficult process and that change from a private to public company is wrenching. There has to be a natural bias against climbing this particular mountain unless one has to do so. Secondly, there are a large number of secure, strong mutual enterprises with currently adequate capital resources for future growth and development. But I believe that history will show the mutual form was too limiting in the developing global insurance market and, in that sense, that the mutual form of enterprise has become an anachronism. Furthermore, mutual-to-stock conversions are a one-way street; it is unlikely there will be any movements back. What I expect is that there will be a slow, but steady, reduction in the number of mutual companies through mergers of mutuals (an easier process) or mutual-to-stock conversions and that by the year 2025 there will be only a handful of mutual companies remaining.

REFERENCES

Kelley, Bruce G. "Stocking a Mutual Insurance Company. The Regulatory Experience." *Federation of Insurance and Corporate Counsel Quarterly,* Fall, 1979.

Section 7312. "Reorganization of a Domestic Mutual Life Insurer into a Domestic Stock Life Insurer." *New York Insurance Laws.* NILS Publishing Company, 1989.

Society of Actuaries. "Report of the Task Force on Mutual Life Insurance Company Conversion." *Transactions of the Society of Actuaries,* 1987.

3 BANKING AND INSURANCE: A BANKING INDUSTRY PERSPECTIVE

Anthony M. Santomero
Richard King Mellon Professor of Finance
Deputy Dean
The Wharton School
University of Pennsylvania

Banks have designs on the insurance industry -- that's the perspective of many in the financial service industry. The evidence seems clear. Money center institutions have been pushing for insurance powers at the national level. They have convinced state banking authorities, such as those in Delaware, to permit bank holding companies to have the right to market insurance nationwide. And in Europe, there is a full-scale conglomeration of universal banking and the insurance industry.[1]

This paper will attempt to explain why the industry wants access to the insurance area and how it is likely to attempt to enter this market. It will take the opportunity to offer the perspective of the banking

---

The author would like to thank David Cummins for helpful suggestions.

[1] The discussion here will center upon the US financial structure. Those interested in the European experience are referred to Steinherr and Huveneers (1989), or Dermine (1990).

industry on this subject and explain that industry's views on the evolution of the financial service industry and its place in it.

This will be accomplished in several steps. First, it will review the evolutional history of the commercial banking firm to explain what it has been through since the landmark legislation of the Great Depression and how this transition has shaped the industry's view of appropriate financial structure and the need for evolutionary change. Next, it will recount the reasons for its interest in insurance products, and by extension, insurance companies themselves. Here, the reasons why the banking industry sees these products as part of a bank's portfolio will be discussed, as well as the perceived efficiency gains and organizational issues facing the combination of banking and insurance products within a broader financial service institution. Finally, the paper will analyze the public policy issues related to fair competition between industries, and so-called level playing fields. In effect, the question of whether or not the merger of banking and insurance activity will prove destabilizing to the financial markets and the financial structure will be addressed.

I offer these insights, not as a Christian entering the lion's den, nor as an emissary of a barbarian tribe to the civilization in its path. Rather, it is the author's view that it is important for the insurance industry to understand the perspective of the U.S. banking industry. The latter has been through much since the Great Depression, and has been on a path of change since the middle of this century. The marketplace cannot ignore these changes in its franchise value, nor the political agenda that the banking industry brings to bear on the issue of the distribution and underwriting of insurance.

This banking perspective is a worthy counterpoint to the insurance companies' view of the problem. As the latter looks to the evolution of insurance products, it describes itself increasingly as part of the financial service industry. Over the past several decades, life insurance firms have evolved from simple firms with the limited product line of whole-life into financial firms that have interest in products in various parts of the financial industry. The latter have been traditionally labelled securities activities, financial market products, commercial and mortgage banking, and underwriting. The broader insurance industry views this evolution as a natural outgrowth of its comparative advantages which includes asset management skills, substantial financial resources, and a large customer base.

Commercial banks also view their expansion into securities and, more recently, insurance products as a natural outgrowth of their expertise and market niche. However, they see their position as much more vulnerable than that of their colleagues in the insurance industry. The latter entered the associated markets for diversification reasons. They added product lines to extend their success and influence; to deepen their customer penetration. The banking industry, by contrast, moved toward product expansion to follow its customers and to prevent further market share shrinkage. It views itself as evolving out of necessity, rather than opportunity.

In the most recent debate concerning appropriate banking powers, the insurance industry has used this weakness in the underlying banking market and its effects on bank performance and balance sheets to its advantage. It has successfully argued against the expansion of powers on the grounds that the insurance industry, which until recently has been a model of stability, did not need these barbarian hordes entering its industry. They would only disrupt it and make it less stable as barbarians always do. Yet, in its zeal to protect its franchise, it has missed a subtle yet critical point--the banking industry has little choice. They cannot return to its own territory of deposit-gathering and simple lending. This market has declined in size and profitability. There is simply not enough space for them there. They search for a new set of products because the old markets have eroded and their customers have moved elsewhere.

Recognizing this doesn't make their case any stronger. And, one may still choose to argue in favor of segmentation. However, it does make their argument more compelling, both to those in the banking industry and to the public policymakers who concern themselves with the stability of our banking and financial industry.

1. The Evolution of the U.S. Banking System

Let us begin by recounting the evolution of the U.S. banking system over the recent past. This will serve as an opening perspective as to why banks have changed and how they have come to view both the insurance and the securities industries as areas of potential growth. The U.S. depository institutions in general and commercial banks specifically have gone through a period of transition from highly regulated firms to ones with fewer constraints on both their product and geographic markets. Let us review how this all occurred.

Product Market Expansion of Commercial Banks

The mid-twentieth century commercial banking structure can be traced back to the Glass-Steagall Act of 1933. More properly titled the Banking Act of 1933, it separated both commercial and investment banking and was a reaction to the financial collapse of the period. As such, it is the root of product regulation. The Act effectively established product market barriers to entry in the commercial and investment banking businesses by separating deposit-taking activity from securities underwriting. It divided a once-combined industry by severely restricting product lines that could be offered by commercial banks and forbidding banking activity within their investment banking counterparts. After much debate, trust activity, which was also subject to divestiture, was retained by the commercial banking sector.

The reasons for this split up are hotly contested. Some saw it as necessary to gain financial stability. As such, they took a public policy position that separate financial institutions would be more stable and provide a better financial environment for industrial growth. Others seized the opportunity of financial crisis to gain competitive advantage and monopoly position.[2]

In the subsequent decade little was done to challenge this regulatory structure surrounding the banking industry, as the economy of the 1930s and the following war period did not lend itself to experimentation. If anything, this era was one of consolidation of regulatory control and restrictions. It was during this period that Congress passed the McCarran-Ferguson Act which specifically granted states the authority to regulate insurance activities, for example. Thus, it was not until the early 1960s that banking firms tried to broaden their markets through product expansion. At first these innovations were limited to offering negotiable certificates of deposit and commingled trust activity. Once begun, however, the process accelerated, but always within the severe regulatory restrictions on bank-allowable activity. The advent of the holding company form led to substantive relief and flexibility. Then, banks wishing to expand their activity could do so

---

[2] There remains considerable debate over the facts surrounding the Depression era financial collapse, and the role played by banking institutions in the crisis. See Benston (1990), and Saunders (1985).

through the establishment of a holding company which transcended the restrictions and regulations that were relevant to the wholly owned banking subsidiaries. Mortgage banking activity and off-shore lending quickly expanded. However, these firms were not granted exemption from the restrictive regulations associated with insurance powers. Therefore, their participation was excluded from the subsequent growth of the insurance industry.

The 1956 passage of the Bank Holding Company Act gave the Federal Reserve Board the authority to determine the permissible activities (products) of these multibank holding companies. To some, this was seen as the first step in the regulators' attempt to control the expansion of this form of financial firm. This was indeed the case for insurance which was formally prohibited from allowable activity both in the banking subsidiary and of any other subsidiary of the bank holding company. However, many banks exploited a loophole in the law and maintained a one-bank holding company structure which allowed continued expansion of their securities activities without regard to national regulatory approval. The 1970 Amendment closed this last loophole by restricting one-bank holding companies to adhere to all provisions of the 1956 Bank Holding Company Act. This new law enabled the Federal Reserve Board to maintain closer control over the activities of commercial bank holding companies, which were in turn restricted to those product areas that were consistent with or equivalent to the business of banking. Yet, to a large extent, the law sanctioned the use of a holding company structure to broaden bank activity into the securities arena. Insurance products, long prohibited, remained beyond the reach of both the bank itself and its newly found holding company parent.

As the trend toward securities activity expansion continued, the movement towards the elimination of the boundary of the commercial and investment banking moved onward. The product lines of these two parts of the financial services industry were becoming more intertwined. Investment banks expanded into a relatively large segment of the retail banking market with the introduction of money market mutual funds, cash management accounts (CMAs), and most recently nonbank-banks. Likewise, commercial banks have expanded their activities in private placements, corporate finance, and commercial paper. Money center banks were the most aggressive, but major regional firms have also garnered an appreciable market share.

At the beginning of the 1990s, then, the U.S. industry is quite different than it had been only fifty years earlier. Banks have expanded through holding company structures to a substantially larger product area. This includes a wider array of corporate banking services, and a larger set of retail customers. The former products, operating through a subsidiary of the bank or holding company, offered commercial clients advice, the *de facto* underwriting of commercial paper, and private placement, to mention just a few. These groups, commonly referred to as a Capital Markets Division, looked increasingly like an investment banking subsidiary. At the consumer level, expanded liability products aimed at a broader segment of household savings flourished, as did trust and investment services. On the credit side, open lines of credit, credit cards, and mortgages of various types all added to the bankers' options.

However, this did not end the industry's evolution. Banks continued to push the boundaries of Glass-Steagall in their move to become full-service institutions. This received a substantial boost by interpretations of the 1933 Act which would allow the major banks to be engaged in limited security underwriting business through affiliates. On June 13, 1988, the Supreme Court let stand the Federal Reserve Board's approval for commercial bank affiliates to underwrite commercial paper, municipal revenue bonds and securities backed by mortgages and consumer debt under the condition that a bank affiliate's underwriting be limited to a small percentage of the affiliate's gross revenue. The ruling was based on the interpretation of the Banking Act which prohibits bank affiliation with firms that are "principally engaged" in securities activities. The percentage limits on underwriting which would keep bank affiliates from being "principally engaged" in securities became the determining factor on permissible association. In 1991 this interpretation was expanded to include the underwriting of equity as permissible activity as well. Although these new powers currently may be useful only to the largest banks, which can develop huge affiliates engaging in non-banking activities, many banks are already directly affected by this ruling and others have announced plans for such security underwriting activity.

Expansion of Geographic Markets

The control of geographic expansion of commercial banks is traced to the 1927 McFadden Act in which the historical tradition of state's right over the allowable expansion of commercial banks was reaffirmed. The 1956 Douglas Amendment of the Bank Holding Company Act continued the deference to state policy on geographic expansion of both nationally- and state-chartered institutions. Specifically, it indicated that out-of-state expansion could not occur unless the host state expressly permitted such entry. The 1960 Bank Merger Act continued the tradition of state's right on this issue. Together, these three Acts had effectively erected barriers to entry in interstate banking by prohibiting banks from: operating branches outside their home state (McFadden Act); purchasing banks outside their home state unless the laws of this acquired bank's state expressly permit such an acquisition (Douglas Amendment); and, by establishing guidelines for the approval of mergers between federally insured banks (Merger Act).

Large bank holding companies wishing to expand their geographic presence were forced to do so through holding company non-bank subsidiaries which would provide a variety of services across the state lines. These services were offered through facilities such as loan production offices (LPOs), international branches referred to as Edge Act offices, as well as a variety of bank holding company nonbank subsidiaries that range from leasing companies and real estate appraisal firms to investment management groups that provided trust services.

As this process of non-bank product expansion continued, the basic vehicle of financial product distribution began to change. Telecommunication and electronics began to replace brick and mortar as a delivery system of retail products. An example of the technology-driven changes in the delivery of retail products is the emergence of the ATM which expanded the potential service area beyond arbitrary branching restrictions. Yet, branching remained the domain of state legislation and was largely restricted to intrastate limits.

State control was nearly complete; yet it was eroding. Legislation passed in 1960 and 1966 which permitted bank mergers that provide benefits to the community which outweigh the potential competitive aspects of a merger. The Bank Merger Act provided the Justice Department with a basis for developing compromise guidelines to be employed in evaluating bank merger proposals. In addition, the emergency provisions of the Garn-St. Germain Act of 1982 provided that banks could cross state boundaries to acquire failing institutions under certain circumstances. This was the first of a growing number of areas in which the previously sacred state boundary began to be crossed in a new wave of mergers. The once-clear limitation of geographic expansion, made official in the Douglas Amendment to the McFadden Act, underwent significant erosion over the next decade. This development added new dimensions and opportunities to the geographic expansion potential of the bank holding company.

The year 1975 was the beginning of formal state legislation which changed the course of interstate banking. Then, Maine enacted the first state law permitting general entry of out-of-state banking units. The result was a period of rapid acquisition of Maine holding companies. Seeing the results of this experiment, additional states did not follow Maine's lead until seven years later. At that point both New York and Massachusetts passed interstate banking laws. The latter, however, was considerably different from the former. While New York authorized out-of-state bank activity within its borders without reciprocity, Massachusetts established a regional banking statute, providing access on a limited basis according to the home state of the holding company. Litigation followed quickly, with the future of regional pacts subject to considerable debate. On June 10, 1985, the Supreme Court of the United States delivered its opinion on the Northeast Bancorp case with an 8-0 court ruling upholding regional banking. The result is that less than a handful of states have not enacted legislation which allows some kind of interstate activity for banks. For those that have, the results of opening up their borders have been immediate, in some cases with substantial cross-boundary acquisitions and regionalization. This has led the Treasury to propose the complete elimination of state restrictions. Their proposal, more radical than the action of the recent past, would allow both bank acquisition and bank branch expansion across state lines. In essence, it would call an end to the history of state authority over bank location decisions.

Understanding Recent Banking Industry Experience

As is evident from the above review, much has been changing on the commercial banking scene. The old lines dividing commercial from investment banking are quickly eroding. State boundaries too have fallen to regional banking trends and the quick evolution to interstate banking. This is a fairly idiosyncratic experience brought about by the historical structure and regulation of commercial banking. Yet, the forces that led to the decline in the regulation of both product and geography are important to understand. Appreciating them is a prerequisite to understanding the institutional evolution reported.

The motive forces behind the evolution of the commercial banking system appear to center around two fundamental issues. First, the product line offered to the industry's natural constituents, firms and households, can not be arbitrarily segmented across industry lines. The attempts by bank regulators to do so were inherently inefficient and opened the way for economic forces consistent with an expansion in the product line offered by various financial entities. Second, technology ultimately made geography less meaningful as a constraint on the delivery system of financial services. This led to an inevitable trend to expand product markets and substituted technology, telecommunications or mail service for physical space. In most cases, this has resulted in increased competition and a reduction in the number of competitors in the industry as a whole.

In terms of the first of these forces, it should have been apparent as early as 1933 that the arbitrary division of products offered to the corporate sector was doomed to failure. As the previous sections recount, banks sought to expand their product menu to satisfy customer needs. This was done first by an expansion into investment banking areas with longer duration, such as private placements and venture pools. It was followed by a realization that a substantial portion of investment banking activity was essentially a substitute for the lending function even at the short end of the maturity spectrum. Commercial paper facilitation and Euromarket syndication are clear cases of loan alternatives into which commercial banks have sought entrance.

It should be pointed out that commercial banks were not the predators in this expanding product-line process. Indeed, it could be argued that our investment banking community, subject to much less explicit regulation, was the first to see the opportunity to expand its product franchise into commercial banking products. Their success led to a further decline in the already small position of commercial banks in the American financial system. Junk bonds, commercial paper, and venture capital pools were the product alternatives used by investment banking firms to enter the traditional bank market of major industrial lending. And these were successful. Their position was further advanced by the process of securitization in which a substantial portion of standard bank portfolios could be initiated and sold without the need of a depository source.[3]

The result of this confrontation between the two divided parts of the banking industry was the virtual elimination of the division proposed

---

[3] For a good review of this evolution, see Litan (1991) or Carlson and Fabozzi (1992).

in the Glass-Steagall Act. Major participants are no longer defined along industry lines, but by their chosen strategy of market concentration. In commercial lending, Goldman Sachs, Bankers Trust, and Morgan Guaranty are more alike than are regional and money center commercial banks, for example.

At the consumer level the same process was at work. Increasingly, household portfolio choice was viewed as hampered by arbitrary restrictions along industry activity lines. The simple savings account gave way to a complex array of portfolio options, only a few of which were previously viewed as allowable activities for commercial banks. Institutions which refused to innovate found themselves losing household market share to a securities industry that adapted well to the consumer's desire for participation in a wider array of debt instruments and access to the equity market. Mutual funds, money market funds, tax-deferred or tax-exempt instruments all developed as alternatives to the previous rather staid and increasingly obsolete bank savings vehicles. Banks had little choice but to evolve so as to follow their customers' needs for greater savings vehicle flexibility.

At the same time, technology was changing the face of the industry and its delivery system. Corporate banking shifted from a simple single-bank relationship and passive corporate finance to unbundled product marketing. Rollover financing directly from the market substituted for bank seasonal borrowing, as lenders were linked more easily with the corporate treasurer's office. Cash management moved from manual systems to on-line real-time cash controls.

On the consumer side, the telephone became a substitute for location in retail deposit gathering. Home banking, wire transfer and the mail box slowly replaced the teller line. In a search for higher yields, portfolios shifted from one bank to another, or from banks to their counterparts in the mutual funds industry or the brokered deposit market.

Credit instruments also evolved. Spearheaded by some aggressive banking firms looking for market share and a different distribution network, electronic banking, credit cards, and point-of-sale products developed. In each case the institution offering the new product saw it as an opportunity to harness new technology and substitute telecommunications for geographic presence. This in turn led to increased concentration of certain product lines as well as emphasis on off-site operation centers to achieve low-cost production. As location became less central, the need for efficient production increased. In many cases the least cost producer was not the banking firm or even part of the banking industry. Accordingly, here, too, market share was lost to aggressive yet efficient competitors from the securities industry. Once again the evolution meant a decline in bank influence and market share.

In all, the above story tells an interesting tale. Banks had been put into a narrow box as a result of the Great Depression. Glass-Steagall, the Bank Holding Company Act, and state's rights had restricted their ability to evolve. They circumvented these restrictions over time through regulatory avoidance and financial manipulation. Through the development of the bank holding company and the evolution of products, they have increasingly moved into the securities industry.

At the same time insurance firms have converted themselves into diversified financial firms. Beginning as a relatively simple part of the financial market, they have changed their product line and innovated, at times aggressively, responding to open market opportunities. While the bank's market share of all intermediary balances has declined from more than 50% to less than a third over the last forty years[4], balances held in pension funds and insurance companies have experienced no such decline. Just as the banking industry examined areas of the securities industry for an opportunity to regain their customers, their balance sheets, and their profitability, they see the insurance industry as a direct competitor and a potentially interesting area into which to expand.

2. The Interest of Banks in Insurance Activity

It is not sufficient to indicate that banks see insurers as competitors and wish to expand into an insurance-type product. One must be more explicit both about what their goals are in this segment of the financial market and how they may choose to achieve them. In fact, much has been written about this issue in the insurance literature.

The general consensus in this literature is that banks wish to engage in the distribution of insurance. According to this line of reasoning, their goal is to increase fee income to improve the return on capital of their basic banking business. Articles such as Pritchett (1990), Felgran (1985), and Korczwk (1987) are representative of this view. They indicate that banks are most interested in competing with the insurance agency function to gain non-interest income. They have little interest or

---

[4] Abel and Bernanke (1992), Table 17.1.

comparative advantage in underwriting. They prefer life to casualty.

However, this perspective on the banking industry's interest in insurance is less than complete. It misses the fundamental lesson of banking history that is recounted above: banks want and need added products. This is true for two reasons. First, their basic position in the financial industry is contracting. Their attempts to broaden the product lines for their customers are attempts to stem this decline. Second, they are interested in more than just fee income. The distribution business which displaces a free-standing, expensive independent broker system is just their first foray into insurance products. Their goal is to cross-sell corporate customers and their indigenous consumer groups into a broader array of products that are both sold and underwritten by the banking organization.

Pundits are correct in arguing that the first step in this strategy is the use of the bank's franchise to cross-sell insurance products. The feasibility of this portion of the strategy relies on some form of value added, and they have correctly centered attention on the banking firm's ability to achieve substantial economy of scope in distribution costs (see Pritchett (1990)). Here, the key factor that is being exploited is the customer relationship and the distribution system already in place. The first is obvious and has resulted in substantial gains in their market share of credit life. The second is perhaps more important. To the extent that the distribution system is less costly than the independent broker mechanisms in place, it offers substantial cost savings to interested consumers. This has been done before in the financial product market in the discount brokerage area. In that case, low-cost producers, some of whom were bank affiliated, took large market shares from full-cost brokers merely because of a lower cost of distribution.

However, this logic is incomplete. As has been indicated in my previous work on conglomerate firms (Herring and Santomero (1990)), substantial success can be achieved either through such production economies or consumption economies by the end-user. The latter may be referred to as economy of scope in consumption. These economies may arise from a reduction in the search, information, monitoring, and/or transaction costs borne by the end-user of financial products. These may be significantly reduced when several financial products are purchased from the same firm.

The bank presumption is that substantial market inroads are possible because of the combination of lower distribution costs and buyer receptivity to one-stop shopping. The prognosis here may be good. Just as insurance firms expanded into securities products such as savings vehicles and mutual funds, commercial banks believe they can cross-sell their corporate and consumer customers from deposit and loan products into insurance. It remains to be seen if this is, in fact, true.[5]

However, bankers also have other designs on the insurance business. The underwriting function offers the insurance industry a very substantial pool of assets under management. Banks have learned through their development of trust departments and their non-bank competitors' growing activity in investment management, that these resources have substantial profit potential. Further, they view themselves as equally astute in the allocation of such assets--recent evidence notwithstanding. Accordingly, it seems unlikely that their corporate designs are on agency activity only. They clearly wish to be in the underwriting business.

Which products offer the most attraction? There are three areas of substantial interest to the banking industry. First, tax-based savings products such as annuities, and various counterparts to pension funds and retirement assets are the most attractive. Actuarial risk is minimal and could even be subcontracted. On the other hand, assets are substantial. We have seen early evidence of this in the annuity business. In addition, bank trust departments and their mutual fund counterparts in the securities industry have been aggressive in their attempts to manage/advise/distribute retirement funds. Commercial bankers clearly see these tax-based products as an area of substantial potential growth for their portfolio, either offered directly by the bank or through an affiliate.

Their next goal will obviously be the life-products area in general. Here again, actuarial risk is well defined and potential assets are a key attraction. The bank's ability to cross-sell to their indigenous retail deposit base is perhaps greatest in this product line as well.

A key question is whether or not the industry has any interest in the underwriting of non-life insurance products. Here the issue is much less clear. Servicing costs are high, profits are highly volatile and the required expertise is difficult to acquire. In addition, potential conflict associated with contesting claims has the most down-side risk to the bank's own franchise value. This suggests that they will not enter the

---

[5] The issue here is less than completely clear. As multiple products are distributed through the same network, expertise declines and efficiency may be lost. See Herring and Santomero (1990).

casualty business very quickly. It is more likely that they will distribute such products on a fee-based or shared-profit basis along the lines envisioned by insurance industry experts. However, the flexibility of a holding company umbrella may offer sufficient market segmentation of product recognition to encourage some institutions to acquire existing firms so as to distribute affiliate products under separate label.

In all, the designs of the banking business are fairly broad-based. They spring from the same features which led them to actively, though belatedly, expand into the securities industry. The commercial industry has both a customer base and a distribution network that requires an array of products which is much broader than the simple banking franchise.

3. Mechanism of Affiliating Banking and Insurance

If banking firms were allowed to enter the insurance industry, what organizational form would they use? The Treasury Proposal[6] suggested the expansion of banking activity into insurance through the use of a Financial Service Holding Company. This concept is essentially equivalent to a broadened version of a Bank Holding Company which was permitted by the 1970 amendment to the 1956 Bank Holding Company Act. Accordingly, the industry would find it quite easy to function with a separate insurance affiliate. In addition, the banking industry has had a long tradition of separation between Trust activity and on-balance sheet lending and deposit-gathering. Given regulatory concerns over conflicts of interest and the independence of the commercial banking unit, it is most likely that any attempt to expand into the insurance industry would be accomplished through the use of a dedicated subsidiary of the financial conglomerate. Financial independence, firewalls, and limited liability could easily be established to segment financially the fortunes of this subsidiary from others.[7]

However, from the perspective of the insurance subsidiary, it

---

[6] For a complete description of the Treasury Proposal submitted to Congress in 1991, see Garsson (1991).

[7] For the banking industry's view of firewalls as efficient mechanisms of financial separation, see Haraf (1990).

should be noted that symmetry is not endorsed by either the Federal Reserve or the FDIC. To regulators charged with maintaining the stability of the banking industry, financial subsidiaries of the Bank Holding Company represent resources which ought to be available to the banking firm. Accordingly, they have argued that any and all assets ought to be made available to support the banking unit. This is the "source of strength" argument which has been invoked in a number of circumstances in the banking industry.[8] On the other hand, non-banking subsidiaries of the holding company are prohibited by law from drawing on the resources of the banking unit.

The insurance subsidiary, therefore, can only be adversely affected by holding company affiliation, if the bank regulator's view of recourse is permitted to become law. Current legislation is less of a concern. It restricts the "source of strength" argument to affiliated banking firms within the holding company but does not allow the bank or any regulatory body to cross company lines to support the banking unit. However, to the extent that insurance powers are granted, one should expect that "source of strength" legislation would be extended to non-bank affiliates. Such a move would be opposed by insurance regulators, to be sure. To members of the insurance industry and their customers, even the potential of an erosion of the stability of the insurance firm should be viewed with alarm.

Banks, themselves, would not necessarily endorse such a holding company structure if they were in a position to select an organizational form unconstrained by regulation. To most in the industry, the universal bank franchise, and by extension the universal financial firm, offers many positive attributes. They would argue, with some validity, that synergies such as cross-marketing and relationship pricing are enhanced by all products offered by a single entity.

The banking industry, however, fails to argue that the regulatory safety net implicit with the universal bank firm offers them a degree of stability which represents a competitive edge over non-bank competitors. The implicit presence of a government guarantee, which is clearly present in the banking industry, allows them a competitive edge which they would much prefer to transfer to their insurance activity than leave behind. Much has been written on this issue as it relates to the banking industry's expansion into securities activity. Therefore, I will refer

---

[8] See Herring and Santomero (1990) for a discussion of this history.

interested readers to a recent review of this issue in Herring and Santomero (1990).

Beyond the point-counterpoint of the regulatory process, however, the banking industry has two fundamental reasons for preferring less distance between banking and insurance activity. First, to the extent that profits are generated through the same distribution system, an awkward cost-accounting problem develops. Shared distribution networks require transfer prices and profitability divisions which, by SEC regulation, must be accurate but are, in reality, arbitrary. Accordingly, the banking institution would prefer to report on a consolidated basis for all products owned and distributed through its network. Second, as indicated above, the primary motivation for engaging in the underwriting of insurance is to gain access to the funding base associated with these deferred liabilities. To the extent that these are held in separate subsidiaries, questions of cross-firm financial flows immediately develop.

This problem is not dissimilar to those that arise between the trust department of commercial banks and their banking affiliate. So, too, they mirror the issue of the segmentation of mutual fund distribution and firm-financing inherent in large investment banks. As both these cases indicate, legislation which requires the separation of banking and insurance affiliates would be acceptable to the industry but not its first choice.

If history is any guide, the erosion of the division between banking and insurance products and these two industries will continue. However, the convoluted nature of financial firms including complex bank holding companies most likely will continue. Accordingly, we in all probability will see separate insurance subsidiaries of banking firms with associated conflicts over the pricing of financial flows, and allowable cross-firm relationships.

4. The Stability Effects of Joint Activity

From a public-policy perspective, one of the key issues surrounding the expansion of banking firms into other areas of the financial service industry is the effect of such expansion on both bank and financial stability. This fact is recognized by both sides of the debate. Bankers, for their part, argue that expanded bank powers will increase financial stability of the banking firm. This view is supported by a series of studies on the issue. On the other hand, the insurance industry and their counterparts in the securities area have argued that expansion of the bank franchise into allied financial services will increase risk both to the banking firm and to the new area of entry. The arguments here are more judgmental and less based on hard analysis. They tend to look at bank performance over the last decade as proof of incompetence. In addition, they point to the high volatility in the non-bank portion of the financial service industry and argue that such risk is inappropriate for government-insured depository institutions.

A recent study sheds light on this issue. In Santomero and Chung (1992), the riskiness of the three segments of the financial service industry, viz., banking, securities, and insurance, over the second half of the 1980s, is examined at some length. This study has something for everyone in its results. It focuses on the effects of expanded bank powers on both the expected return and riskiness of a financial service firm using market-driven valuation techniques. While the methodology does not examine the possible intangible benefits and risks associated with such an expansion of powers, it does offer some interesting insights on the stability issue.

This study estimated both a return and a risk measure for each industry and constructed hypothetically merged ones. It calculated these estimates from time-series data on the return on equity, its market value and the book value of total firm debts for the banking, securities and insurance firms. These data are easily observable and readily available through Compustat and CRSP tapes. Given that these are market-value data, the results are comparable and do not depend upon accounting data or differential regulatory reporting issues in the three industries.

In estimating riskiness, a theoretical valuation model which comes to the institutions area from the option-pricing literature was employed. According to the option-pricing literature, asset return volatility (σ_A) is a function of the total equity value (E), the promised payments to the debtholders (B) at the time of maturity, (T), the risk-free rate (r), and the market value of total assets (A). In addition, the theory suggests that the market value of assets, A, is a function of the above parameters (E, B, T, and r) and the asset return volatilities, σ_A. Therefore, even though σ_A and A are not observable, both values can be estimated by utilizing these two functional relationships coming from option-pricing theory. [9]

This market-based measure of risk is clearly superior to other risk measures such as variability of the stock returns because the latter measure only shows the volatility of equity value, not the variability of the firm's rate of return on assets. The only conditions for this approach to be valid are that market values provide accurate information about the true economic values and option-pricing theory is a valid valuation technique.

To proceed with this methodology, we first calculated the volatility of the daily rate of return on assets, σ_A, for each sample firm in the separate industries. This permits us to report the riskiness of each subset of the financial industry individually. Then, the volatilities of hypothetical firms created by the merger of hypothetical partners from each industry are calculated to evaluate the risk effect of the expansion of banking firms into non-banking activities. Consistent with previous models of Merton (1977), Ronn and Verma (1986), and the empirical results of Gorton and Santomero (1990), we assumed an annual horizon for the option calculations based on the fact that financial firms are examined each year.[10]

Subject to all of the above, the implied volatilities of the individual firms in each of the currently separate industries, viz., commercial banking, insurance and securities, were calculated. In each industry two subsets are considered. The banking industry is divided into money center and regional banks. The insurance firms include life insurance and property and casualty firms, and the security firms sample is divided into national and regional firms. To obtain average measures

---

[9] The empirical procedure employed follows Ronn and Verma (1986) rather closely. The technical details are presented in Santomero and Chung (1992) pp. 13-15.

[10] There is a real issue in this methodological approach surrounding the appropriate characterization of closure, or failure. If the market value of the assets falls below the total debts, the authorities have to take whatever measures they think are adequate for the situation. They may revive a troubled firm by providing necessary funds; they may liquidate it; or, they may use a "purchase and assumption" method of dealing with the problem institution. The actual estimation of σ_A is affected by their decision concerning the exact point at which closure will be imposed.

for an industry, we averaged the volatilities of the individual firms in each industry using the calculated market values of the assets of individual firms as weights.

Return measures for each sample quarter are obtained by estimating the market-based average return on assets of an individual firm. Then we computed the weighted average return of an industry to examine the profitability of each industry. With these weighted returns and volatilities, we made comparisons of the riskiness between industries, both real and hypothetical ones.[11]

Using the calculated implied volatilities of asset returns, the rates of return, and capitalization rates (equity-to-assets ratios), we estimated another important risk measure. This measure, denoted as Z, is employed elsewhere by Boyd and Graham (1988) and Brewer (1989). Under the assumption that the rates of return are distributed normally, the value of Z indicates the number of standard deviations that the rate of return would have to fall below its expectation in order for the firm to go bankrupt, defined as the situation where losses exceed equity. Therefore, Z can be viewed as an indicator of the probability of bankruptcy in the sense that a higher value of Z indicates a lower probability of failure.[12]

The study used Compustat and CRSP data for a five-year period from 1985 through 1989. The total sample includes 123 BHCs, 45 insurance firms, and 17 security firms. This yields a potential of 123 hypothetical firms created by the random merger with these nonbank firms.

Without belaboring the analytics of the approach, let us proceed to some of its results. Table 1 reports the results of the estimation of riskiness, rates of return, and the Z failure index over the five-year sample. For each industry and the two subdivisions thereof, average

---

[11] For the estimation of asset volatility for the hypothetical firms the procedure involves estimating the daily return on equity for the hypothetical firm using relevant market values. Given this time series and the book value of debt the process proceeds as above.

[12] Even though the rates of return may not be normally distributed, Z can be used as an index of the maximum probability of bankruptcy. This can be demonstrated by employing Chebychev's inequality which relates the maximum probability of failure to the square of the inverse of Z.

TABLE 1
Mean of 20 Quarters from 1985 to 1989 (Unmerged Industries)

Industries	σ_A (Rank)	M_A (Rank)	Z values (Rank)
BHC	1.51	1.24	5.17
MBHC	1.28 (6)	1.00 (5)	4.65 (4)
RBHC	1.69 (5)	1.45 (4)	5.47 (1)
INSU	4.29	3.88	5.25
PINSU	5.86 (1)	5.77 (1)	5.42 (2)
LINSU	3.23 (3)	2.59 (2)	5.05 (3)
SECU	2.08	0.91	3.66
BSECU	1.97 (4)	0.82 (6)	3.71 (5)
RSECU	3.77 (2)	2.35 (3)	3.35 (6)

legend:
BHC   = all bank holding companies
MBHC = money center bank holding companies
RBHC = regional bank holding companies
INS   = all insurance companies
PINSU = property and casualty insurance companies
LINSU = life insurance companies
SEC   = all securities firms
BSECU = large investment and securities firms
RSEC = regional investment and securities firms
σ_A = quarterly mean estimated implied volatility of industry
M_A = quarterly mean rate of return on the estimated market value of assets
Z   = number of standard deviations of asset returns to cause bankruptcy
        based on mean values

performance and rank order are reported. As is clear from the data, the banking industry as a whole was less profitable than the insurance industries in the sample, but somewhat more profitable than their security counterparts. This is primarily due to the poor performance of large securities houses which rank sixth among the subgroups considered.

In terms of riskiness, the implied volatility derived from market prices suggests that the banking industry is substantially more stable than any of its counterparts. Property and casualty firms are the most volatile in the sample, followed by regional security firms, life insurance, and large security houses. Both subcategories of the banking industry exhibit a lower volatility than their counterparts elsewhere in the financial market.

The Z score which measures the underlying riskiness of the firm, incorporating volatility and profitability, is reported in column 3. Here larger values are preferred as the Z score is a measure of the number of standard deviations from failure. Notice that the banking industry as a whole now ranks second somewhat behind the insurance industry but significantly ahead of either group in the securities area. Money center banks perform significantly worse than their regional counterparts as well as the insurance industry as a whole.

In all, the data on individual industry performance are consistent with the conflict presently underway. Insurance firms have exhibited substantially higher returns than their banking counterparts. Accordingly, their franchise proves attractive to the banking firm and, for that matter, the securities industry in general. On the other hand, concerns about stability are well placed. Particularly in the casualty area, volatility is substantially higher in the insurance industry sample than the banking industry counterpart.

In terms of correlation, Table 2 reports the cross-correlation between banking and other non-banking parts of the financial service industry.[13] Notice that returns are positively correlated but not excessively so. In fact, of the eight two-industry correlations, life insurance performs quite well as an added product line within a banking firm.

The study goes on to analyze the hypothetical merger of various parts of the financial services industry and reports the effect of these mergers on returns, riskiness, and failure probability. These results are contained in Table 3.

These data suggest that the merging of insurance and/or securities firms with the banking industry substantially increases the stability of the combined firm. Any pair-wise comparison results in a reduction in implied volatility. On the other hand, extending the insurance industry into banking reduces profitability, as profits of the two sectors are averaged. The analysis comes to a conclusion in the last

---

[13] This correlation can be estimated indirectly from the computed value for A and σ_A for the independent industries and the hypothetically combined ones. See Santomero and Chung (1992), p. 19.

TABLE 2
Mean of 20 Correlation Coefficients of 20 Quarters

Industries	Mean Ranking
BHC-BS	0.324
MBHC-BS	0.3661
RBHC-BS	0.3202
BHC-RS	0.098
MBHC-RS	0.1756
RBHC-RS	0.0918
BHC-PI	0.279
MBHC-PI	0.2863
RBHC-PI	0.2784
BHC-LI	0.182
MBHC-LI	0.1277
RBHC-LI	0.1875

legend:
- hyphenated industries are two-industry hypothetical mergers
- the mean estimate of industry correlation is measured indirectly from estimates of σ_A and A and their values for separate subsectors. See text.

column of this table. Notice that the combined firm is significantly more stable than the independent counterparts. This advantage accrues not only to the banking industry, but also the insurance industry. Taken as a whole, the data suggest that conglomeration of banking and insurance adds to, rather than subtracts from, the stability of the financial service sector. The results relating to public policy are clear. Congress concerned about the Savings and Loan debacle and the continued poor performance of the banking industry would find this stability result a forceful argument in favor of merged activities.

TABLE 3
Mean of 20 Quarters from 1985 to 1989

Industries	σ_A (Rank)	M_A (Rank)	Z Value (Rank)
BHC-LI	1.91(6)	1.78(6)	5.87(5)
MBHC-LI	1.28	1.05	4.98
RBHC-LI	2.16	2.09	6.07
BHC-PI	3.21(2)	3.30(2)	5.89(4)
MBHC-PI	1.77	1.60	5.43
RBHC-PI	3.78	3.96	5.94
BHC-BS	1.69(9)	0.96(10)	4.59(11)
MBHC-BS	1.29	0.96	5.01
RBHC-BS	1.78	0.97	4.52
BHC-RS	1.48(11)	1.31(7)	5.49(7)
MBHC-RS	1.27	1.03	4.81
RBHC-RS	1.63	1.55	5.87
BHC-LI-BS	1.74(8)	1.21(8)	5.24(9)
MBHC-LI-BS	1.33	0.99	5.16
RBHC-LI-BS	1.84	1.26	5.20
BHC-LI-RS	1.87(7)	1.81(5)	6.03(3)
MBHC-LI-RS	1.28	1.07	5.07
RBHC-LI-RS	2.10	2.12	6.23
BHC-PI-BS	2.14(4)	1.78(6)	5.60(6)
MBHC-PI-BS	1.63	1.34	5.46
RBHC-PI-BS	2.27	1.87	5.57
BHC-PI-RS	2.95(3)	3.19(3)	6.10(2)
MBHC-PI-RS	1.71	1.56	5.44
RBHC-PI-RS	3.46	3.82	6.15
BHC-PI-LI-BS-RS	2.06(5)	1.91(4)	6.16(1)
MBHC-PI-LI-BS-RS	1.49	1.38	6.05
RBHC-PI-LI-BS-RS	2.14	2.00	6.23
BHC Alone	1.51(10)	1.24(9)	5.17(10)
MBHC	1.28	1.00	4.65
RBHC	1.69	1.45	5.47
INSU Alone	4.29(1)	3.88(1)	5.25(8)
PI	5.86	5.77	5.42
LI	3.23	2.59	5.05

5. Summary and Conclusion

The previous discussion reviews the continued controversy over the respective places of banks and insurance companies in the financial services industry. This was accomplished with a particular perspective in mind--a banking viewpoint. Some things appear to be clear from this vantage point. First, banks have spent nearly 30 years working to expand their franchise and circumvent restrictive legislation in the United States. They did so in an effort to maintain customer relationships at a time when communications and technology were breaking down their basic franchise. These attempts notwithstanding, the banking industry is relatively smaller now than ever before in the 20th century. Coupled with poor performance, the industry is in trouble and wishes to expand its franchise as a way of both following its customers and obtaining financial viability.

Second, insurance and securities products are natural extensions of the bank's franchise. Indeed, these two industries have increased their fraction of corporate and consumer financial activity over the same period. Accordingly, banks clearly wish to expand in these product areas so as to exploit their distribution system and cross-sell to their existing customers. Ultimately, their true goal is to obtain not only the fee income associated with insurance products but also the funding base that these products represent.

Third, an expansion of the inter-relationships between different parts of the financial services industry would seem to add stability through standard diversification arguments. The data reported here and the general tenor of previous research support this result.

To date, the insurance lobby has been successful in maintaining its position and its franchise in spite of interest by the commercial banking industry in expanding its product line into insurance-related products. Prognosticators agree that the wall between insurance and banking is not likely to be destroyed very soon. Yet, the banking industry has learned much from its past history. As the historical account above illustrates, they have been able to advance their interests at the local level rather effectively. State's rights, once the bane of their existence, has proved to be a boon. Working through state legislatures and courts that support their authority, banks will continue to erode the insurance franchise. Expect their presence to be felt over the near-term.

In the end, the position of the banking industry in the general insurance market will be based not just on its own interests in the area, nor on public policy concerns. The political realities of regulation will dictate the outcome, at least over the longer run. From this vantage point, while the insurance lobby has been quite successful, this success is not sustainable. The ratification of state's rights in the recent ruling in favor of Citicorp illustrates this point. Erosion in their monopoly position is inevitable. In the end, we will come to recognize that banking, insurance, and securities are all parts of the broader financial services industry.

REFERENCES

Abel, A. A. and B. S. Bernanke, *Macroeconomics*, New York, Addison Wesley Publishing, 1992.

Benston, George J., *The Separation of Commercial and Investment Banking: The Glass-Steagall Act Revisited and Reconsidered*, New York, Oxford University Press, 1990.

Brewer III, E., "Relationship Between Bank Holding Company Risk and Nonbank Activity." *Journal of Economics and Business*, 41 (1989), 337-53.

Boyd, J. H. and S. L. Graham, "The Profitability and Risk Effects of Allowing Bank Holding Companies to Merge with Other Financial Firms: A Simulation Study." *Quarterly Review* (Federal Reserve Bank of Minneapolis), 12, (Spring 1988), 3-20.

Carlson, J. H. and F. J. Fabozzi (eds.), *The Trading and Securitization of Senior Bank Loans*, Chicago, Probus Publishing Co., 1992.

Dermine, Jean, *European Banking after 1992*, Oxford: Basil Blackwell, 1990.

Felgran, Steven D., "Banks as Insurance Agencies: Legal Constraints and Competitive Advances." *New England Economic Review*, Sept./Oct. 1985, pp. 37-45.

Garsson, R. M., "Bush Faces an Uphill Battle for His Bank Reform Plan." *American Banker*, February 11, 1991.

Gorton G. and A. M. Santomero, "Market Discipline and Bank Subordinated Debt." *Journal of Money, Credit, and Banking*, 22, No.1 (February 1990), 119-28.

Haraf, W. S., "Separating Banking and Securities: The Social Cost of Regulatory 'Firewalls'," Citicorp, 1990.

Herring, R.J. and A.M. Santomero, "The Corporate Structure of Financial Conglomerates." *Journal of Financial Services Research*, December 1990, 471-497.

Korczyk, Sophie M., "Expanded Bank Powers: Implications for the Insurance Industry," unpublished paper for the Independent Insurance Agents of America, 1987.

Litan, Robert, *The Revolution in U.S. Finance*, Washington, The Brookings Institution, 1991.

Merton, R. C., "An Analytic Derivation of the Cost of Deposit Insurance and Loan Guarantees." *Journal of Banking and Finance*, 1, June 1977, 3-11.

Pritchett, S. Travis, "Banking and Insurance," manuscript, University of South Carolina, 1990.

Ronn, E. and A. Verma, "Pricing Risk-Adjusted Deposit Insurance: An Option-Based Model." *Journal of Finance* XLI, No.4, September 1986, 871-95.

Santomero, A.M., "The Changing Structure of Financial Institutions: A Review Essay." *Journal of Monetary Economics*, September 1989.

Santomero, A.M. and E.C. Chung, "Evidence in Support of Broader Bank Powers." *Journal of Financial Markets, Institutions and Instruments* 1:1992 (formerly Salomon Brothers Monograph series in Finance and Economics).

Saunders, Anthony, "Conflicts of Interest: An Economic View." in *Deregulatory Wall Street Commercial Bank Penetration of the Securities Business*, I. Walter (ed.), New York, J. Wiley and Sons, 1985.

Steinherr, A. and C. Huveneers, "Universal Banks: The Prototype of Successful Banks in the Integrated European Market," Centre for European Policy Studies 2 (1989)

4 THE MYTHS AND REALITY OF LOW-GRADE BONDS

Marshall E. Blume

Howard Butcher III Professor of Financial Management
The Wharton School
University of Pennsylvania

Donald B. Keim

Associate Professor of Finance
The Wharton School
University of Pennsylvania

Abstract

This paper updates through June 1991 the authors' prior research on low-grade bonds. The paper finds further support for the hypothesis that low-grade bonds behave sometimes like high-grade bonds and sometimes like small stocks. Much of the drop in the prices of low-grade bonds in the last half of 1990 and the subsequent increase in the first half of 1991 parallel the price movements of small stocks. Also consistent with our earlier work, the volatility of low-grade bonds is less than that of high-grade corporates or long-term governments. The shorter "duration" of low-grade bonds accounts for this counter-intuitive result.

The authors thank Darren Klein for his excellent research assistance and the Geewax-Terker Research Program in Financial Instruments for financial support.

1. Introduction

The market for low-grade bonds as we know it today began in 1977 with the issuance of 1.1 billion dollars of new issues. Previously in the post-World War II period, virtually all new issues of publicly traded bonds carried an investment grade rating of BBB or higher (in terms of the Standard and Poor's rating system). The important change in 1977 was the issuance of bonds whose initial ratings were below investment grade. No longer were low-grade bonds solely "fallen angels," bonds originally issued with an investment-grade rating but subsequently downgraded to below investment grade.

From 1977 through 1989, the market for low-grade bonds grew dramatically. In 1989 alone, new issues amounted to 24.2 billion dollars, and the outstanding market value of low-grade bonds had grown to 205 billion dollars, representing roughly a quarter of all marketable corporate debt.[1] In 1990 new issues collapsed to 1.4 billion dollars. There has been a modest recovery in 1991 with 3.8 billion dollars of new issues through October 7.[2]

Despite the drop in new underwritings in 1989 and 1990, Merrill Lynch as well as Salomon Brothers estimate that the outstanding supply of low-grade bonds is still over 200 billion dollars, making these bonds a significant asset class.[3] As such, low-grade bonds warrant continued study.

Numerous studies have documented the higher default rates of low-grade bonds in comparison to high-grade bonds,[4] but these results are not surprising. After all, low-grade bonds should have a greater probability of default. These studies of default rates are clearly of interest, but what is ultimately of overriding interest to investors is the effect of

---

[1] Drexel Burnham supplied these estimates.

[2] Merrill Lynch supplied these estimates of new issues for 1990 and 1991.

[3] Recently, redemptions have exceeded new issues, which by itself would reduce the supply. However, the rapid increase in the market value of existing bonds in 1991, a fact documented below, has offset this effect.

[4] Examples include Altman (1987, 1989) and Asquith, Mullins and Wolff (1989).

higher levels of default on the realized returns of low-grade bonds. In a number of previous studies, we have examined some of the characteristics of the returns realized by low-grade bonds.[5] This paper updates these earlier studies through June 1991. The turbulent markets in the last half of 1990 and the first half of 1991 make such an update most relevant at this time.

After a short description of the data, the second section of the paper presents some statistics summarizing the return and volatility characteristics of long-term low-grade bonds, and corresponding statistics for other asset classes. The third section contains an analysis of the covariability of the returns of low-grade bonds and the other assets classes. The fourth section summarizes our findings.

2. Return Statistics for Low-Grade Bonds

A major difficulty in analyzing the returns realized by the low-grade bond universe, particularly for the early years, is obtaining reliable prices. To help overcome this difficulty, both Drexel Burnham Lambert and Salomon Brothers provided us with month-end bid prices for original-issue low-grade bonds covering the years 1982-1988. The bonds included in our index calculations have a face value of $25,000,000 at time of issue, are non-convertible, and have ten or more years to maturity.[6] Thus, the return index for the low-grade bonds discussed in this study should be viewed as a long-term index and not necessarily representative of the short-term low-grade universe.

The index was constructed as follows: We computed the total monthly returns (coupon and capital appreciation) for all bonds in the Salomon and Drexel subsamples.[7] To avoid any bias due to dropping a

---

[5] See Blume and Keim (1987), Blume and Keim (1991) and Blume, Keim and Patel (1991).

[6] When a bond had less than ten years to maturity, it was dropped from our calculations.

[7] For those bonds that appeared in both subsamples, we used the average of the prices in computing these monthly total returns. The total return for a month is the ratio of the end-of-month market price plus accrued interest to the prior end-of-month price plus accrued interest, less one. If a coupon

bond before it defaults, we augmented the basic Drexel-Salomon data files with total returns derived from prices in the S&P Bond Guide for the two months following the deletion of a bond from either the Salomon or Drexel sample.[8] We then combined the individual bond returns with equal weights to arrive at a monthly total return index.

To analyze the realized returns of these bonds before 1982, we collected month-end bond prices for the 1977-1981 period for all bonds satisfying the same criteria as above and listed in the S&P Bond Guide. These monthly prices may be less reliable than those provided to us for the 1982-1988 period, but using these prices allows us to analyze the low-grade bond market from its beginnings in 1977. We did compare indexes constructed from the Drexel-Salomon data and the S&P data over the 1982-1986 period[9] and found a high correlation between these two indexes, suggesting that indexes based upon S&P prices prior to 1982 are

---

was paid during the month, the end-of-month price was increased by the amount of the coupon.

[8] There are 226 bonds used in the construction of our indexes which Drexel or Salomon dropped from their databases, 98 of which were dropped in 1986. The S&P Bond Guide contains the needed price information for 177 of these bonds. A comparison of these added returns for the Salomon database over 1982-85 shows that on average the added monthly returns are 1.2 percent less than the continuing returns in each of the two subsequent months. The returns of the 19 bonds not quoted in the S&P Bond Guide are approximated in any month by the average monthly returns of the continuing bonds less 1.2 percent. For 1986, the average return for the dropped bonds for which price information was available was -8.2 percent for the month following the drop and zero for the subsequent month. For the 30 bonds in 1986 for which price information was unavailable in the Bond Guide, the returns for the first and second months following their elimination were assumed to be -8.2 percent and zero, respectively.

[9] Since we did not collect the payment dates for the S&P bonds, we approximated the bond return as the ratio of the end-of-month market price plus one twelfth of the annual coupon to the prior end-of-month market price, less one.

credible.[10]

For 1989 and later, we did not have data on individual bonds, and thus relied on other sources, For 1989, we used the long-term low-grade bond index published by Drexel to measure monthly returns, and for the eighteen months ending June 1991, we used the long-term low-grade bond index published by Salomon. Both of these indexes are quite similar to our index from 1977 through 1988 in that they are based upon long-term bonds and are properly adjusted for defaults.

For comparison purposes, we employ monthly returns for two stock indexes and two bond indexes published by Ibbotson Associates. The stock indexes are the S&P 500 and a small-stock index. The small-stock index measures the returns of a value-weighted portfolio of NYSE and AMEX stocks in the smallest size quintile as determined by NYSE stocks. The bond indexes are a long-term high-grade corporate bond index, which is identical to the Salomon Brothers index of the same name, and a long-term government bond index with a maturity of approximately 20 years.

Realized Returns

From January 1977 through June 1991, low-grade bonds had an annual compounded rate of return of 10.3 percent (Table 1 and Figure 1). This return is greater than the 8.9 percent realized by long-term government bonds and the 9.8 percent realized by long-term high-grade corporates. The return is less than the 13.8 percent realized by the S&P 500 and the 18.0 percent realized by small stocks. Thus, over these fourteen and a half years, the return on low-grade bonds was between those of the two higher grade bond indexes and those of the two stock indexes.

This relative ranking that we observe for the entire period is sensitive to the time period over which the returns are measured. An examination of the seven successive two-year periods from July 1977 through June 1991 discloses substantial variability in the rankings of realized returns (Table 2). For example, in the first and second two-year periods ending June 1979 and June 1981, the returns of low-grade bonds exceed those of the two other bond indexes and are less than either stock

---

[10] See Blume and Keim (1987) for an extended discussion of this comparative analysis.

TABLE 1

Summary Statistics of Returns for Various Asset Categories
January 1977 - June 1991

	Annual Compounded Return	Monthly			
		Mean Return	Standard Return	Adjusted Standard Deviation[1]	Auto-correlation ρ_1
Long-Term Government Bonds	8.9	0.78	3.62	3.85	0.07
Long-Term High-Grade Corporate Bonds	9.8	0.81	3.31	3.74	0.15
Long-Term Low-Grade Bonds	10.3	0.86	2.88	3.52	0.27
S&P 500	13.8	1.19	4.59	4.76	0.04
Small Stocks	18.0	1.56	5.67	6.54	0.18

[1]Stale prices can induce positive but spurious autocorrelation in the indices of returns, biasing downward the estimated standard deviation of monthly returns. To examine the magnitude of this bias, the monthly standard deviations were adjusted in a two-step procedure: First, annualize the estimated monthly standard deviation, taking into account the autocorrelation. If σ^2 is the monthly variance and the first order autocorrelation is ρ_1 with all other autocorrelations zero, the variance of the sum of 12 monthly returns is $\sigma^2(12 + 22\rho_1)$. Thus, multiplying the monthly standard deviation by $(12 + 22\rho_1)^{1/2}$ yields an annual standard deviation that takes into account the first order serial correlation. Second, divide by the $\sqrt{12}$ to reexpress this annual standard deviation in monthly units. If the second order autocorrelation is ρ_2 and all high order autocorrelations are zero, the multiplying constant is $(12 + 22\rho_1 + 20\rho_2)^{1/2}$.

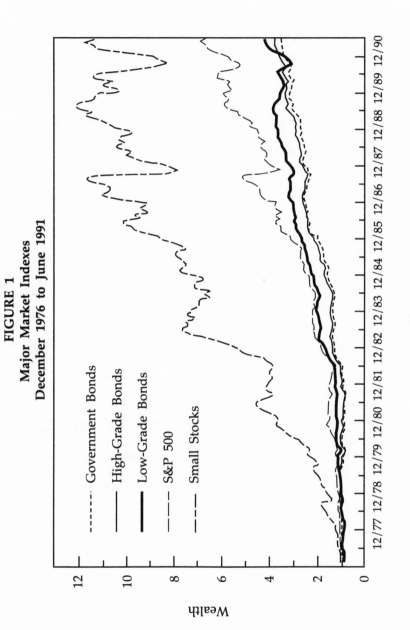

FIGURE 1
Major Market Indexes
December 1976 to June 1991

Government Bonds
High-Grade Bonds
Low-Grade Bonds
S&P 500
Small Stocks

Wealth

Year

12/77 12/78 12/79 12/80 12/81 12/82 12/83 12/84 12/85 12/86 12/87 12/88 12/89 12/90

0   2   4   6   8   10   12

TABLE 2
Annual Returns and Standard
Deviations for Successive Two-Year Periods

Date	Long-Term Government Bonds	Long-Term High-Grade Corporate Bonds	Long-Term Low-Grade Bonds	S&P 500	Small Stocks
A. Annual Compounded Returns					
7/1977 - 6/1979	2.3	3.1	4.7	6.7	31.6
7/1979 - 6/1981	-7.0	-7.8	0.6	18.8	51.8
7/1981 - 6/1983	21.7	24.4	24.2	19.4	29.5
7/1983 - 6/1985	15.2	15.4	13.5	11.9	0.9
7/1985 - 6/1987	17.0	15.6	13.1	30.3	18.7
7/1987 - 6/1989	11.8	12.3	10.5	5.9	2.7
7/1989 - 6/1991	6.8	8.3	4.4	11.8	-1.6
B. Standard Deviations of Monthly Returns					
7/1977 - 6/1979	1.5	1.3	2.0	4.0	7.2
7/1979 - 6/1981	5.1	5.1	4.3	4.6	5.3
7/1981 - 6/1983	4.8	4.7	3.4	4.8	5.3
7/1983 - 6/1985	3.6	3.6	2.1	3.5	4.3
7/1985 - 6/1987	4.1	2.5	1.8	4.8	4.3
7/1987 - 6/1989	2.9	2.5	1.8	6.0	7.1
7/1989 - 6/1991	2.2	1.6	3.9	4.6	5.7

Source: From 1977 through 1988, the bonds underlying the low-grade bond index are all non-convertible with face value at time of issue of greater than $25 million and with time to maturity of at least ten years from the date on which any return is calculated. The returns for the individual bonds from 1982 through 1988 are based upon bid prices from Drexel Burnham Lambert and Salomon Brothers and prior to 1982 upon prices from the *S&P Bond Guide*. The return indexes from 1977 through 1988 are averages of these returns by month. For 1989, Drexel calculated a monthly return index using bid prices in virtually the same way as the 1977-1988 indexes were calculated, and this index was used to extend the sample through 1989. The returns from January 1990 through June 1991 are derived from the Salomon Brothers long-term bond index for low-grade bonds. The returns for (1) the S&P 500, (2) a value-weighted portfolio of common stocks in the smallest size quintile on the NYSE, (3) the Salomon Brothers index of long-term high-grade (rated A and above) corporate bonds, and (4) long-term (approximately twenty years to maturity) government bonds are from Ibbotson Associates.

index. Note that the annual returns on small stocks are extremely high during these two periods (31.6 percent and 51.8 percent, respectively).

Similarly, in the third two-year period ending in June 1983, low-grade bonds earned 24.2 percent---slightly less than the 24.4 percent for corporates and the 29.5 percent for small stocks, but greater than the 21.7 percent for governments and the 19.4 percent for the S&P 500. In the fourth and sixth two-year period ending in June 1985 and in June 1989, however, the returns on low-grade bonds exceeded the returns for both stock indexes, and the high-grade bond returns exceeded the low-grade bond returns. In contrast, in the fifth two-year period ending June 1987, low-grade bonds realized 13.1 percent---the lowest rate of returns of the five asset classes. In the last period ending June 1991, small stocks earned the lowest returns (-1.6 percent), followed by low-grade bonds (4.4 percent).

In sum, over the entire fourteen and a half years from January 1977 through June 1991, the realized annual returns on long-term low-grade bonds exceeded the corresponding returns on both long-term governments and long-term high-grade corporates, but were less than the returns on the two stock indexes. However, there was wide variability in the rankings of the returns of these various asset classes by subperiod.

Relative Volatility

For the January 1977 through June 1991 period, the volatility of monthly returns of low-grade bonds as measured by their standard deviation is less than the volatility of any of the four comparison asset categories (Table 1). Specifically, the standard deviation of monthly returns is 2.88 percent for low-grade bonds, 3.31 for long-term high-grade corporates, 3.62 for long-term governments, 4.59 percent for the S&P 500, and 5.67 percent for small stocks.

Unlike the relative rankings of realized returns, there is comparative stability in the relative rankings of the standard deviations of monthly returns across the asset classes (Table 2). In each of the seven successive two-year periods ending in June 1991, the standard deviation of the returns for low-grade bonds was less than that of either equity index. In all but two of the seven two-year periods, the standard deviation of monthly returns for low-grade bonds is less than that for either of the two higher grade bond indexes. The two exceptions are the periods from July 1977 through June 1979 and from July 1989 through June 1991.

The finding that the monthly volatility of low-grade bonds is less than that of high-grade corporates or governments over the extended period from 1977 through June 1991 and for five of the seven successive two-year periods may seem counterintuitive. As it turns out, sound economic reasons can account for this result. Before delving into these reasons, we shall first dispose of a statistical explanation---namely, that "stale" prices cause a downward bias in the estimated volatility of low-grade bonds and that this bias is greater for low-grade bonds than for other asset classes.

The effect of including an occasional "stale" price in the calculation of an index is to smooth the returns of that index and thus to reduce the estimated standard deviation. To illustrate, suppose that the general level of interest rates moves up, so that all bonds experience losses. If it takes a transaction to change the recorded price and if not all of the bonds in an index trade, some of the bonds will have recorded prices that do not reflect their "true" current prices. Thus, an index of bonds calculated with both current true prices and old "stale" prices will not drop as much as it should since the recorded "stale" prices are greater than their unrecorded "true" prices. The effect is to spread a change in market value artificially over two or more periods, reducing the apparent volatility of the index.

If "stale" prices are more common with low-grade bonds, a statistical bias might explain the apparent lower standard deviations of low-grade bonds. An adjustment to the estimated standard deviations allows us to explore this possibility. If the changes in prices from one month to the next are uncorrelated, the autocorrelations of the calculated index are a measure of the effect of "stale" prices and can be used to make the required adjustment. In this framework, a positive autocorrelation indicates the presence of stale prices.

The first order autocorrelation coefficients are positive for all asset classes, but greatest for low-grade bonds. Adjusting for "stale" prices using these positive autocorrelations leads to increased estimates of the volatility of the returns of all asset groups but with the greatest increase for the low-grade bond index. Yet, the adjusted volatility of low-grade bonds for the 1977-1991 period is still less than that of either governments or corporates, although the gap is considerably narrowed (Table 1).

We now entertain several economic reasons for the apparent lower volatility of low-grade bonds in comparison to the other two types of bonds. First, we explore potential differences in the durations of the different bond indexes. Duration measures the sensitivity of bond prices to interest rate movements. Although all of the bond indexes are long-term indexes, the durations of the indexes differ. Importantly, the duration of the low-grade bond index is less than that of either the long-term high-grade corporate index or the long-term government index. There are several reasons. First, the time to maturity of low-grade bonds in our index is less than the time to maturity for either of these two indexes. At the end of 1988, the time to maturity of the low-grade bonds in our index was slightly less than 15 years, in contrast to the maturity of 20 years for these two indexes. Second, the coupons of the low-grade bonds in our universe are greater than those of the governments or corporates. This shorter maturity and the larger coupons result in a shorter duration that will make the returns of low-grade bonds less sensitive to general interest rate movements than the returns of the comparison bonds.

There are still other reasons for the relatively low duration of the index of low-grade bonds. First, low-grade bonds are more likely to be called than long-term governments or even long-term high-grade corporate bonds since low-grade bonds typically have less call protection than these other two type of bonds. Some low-grade bonds have no call protection at all, and some are callable after as short a period of three years. In contrast, long-term governments are callable only within the five years preceding maturity or not callable at all. High-grade corporates usually have a five- or a ten-year call protection period. Thus, if interest rates increase, low-grade bonds are more likely to be called, which reduces their relative duration.

Additionally, a corporation may decide to call its low-grade bonds even if there were no changes in the general level of interest rate. The credit quality of an issuer of a low-grade bond may improve, allowing a refinancing of the bond at lower interest rate. Also, a corporate issuer of low-grade bonds may decide at some point, quite apart from changes in interest rates, to improve the financial quality of its balance sheet by replacing the debt with equity.

Finally, although not formally the same as a call, an issuer of a low-grade bond may default, which reduces the effective life of the bond and thus its "duration." As long as the occurrences of defaults are uncorrelated across bonds, defaults themselves will not have a significant impact upon the volatility of an index although the presences of such defaults will reduce the expected return of an index.

For all of these reasons, a comparison of the volatility of low-grade bonds to the volatility of the other two bond asset classes does not hold everything constant. A prior study[11] derived an index of government bonds adjusted to have the same "duration" as the low-grade bond index in terms of coupons and call features. With this adjustment, the volatility of the government bond index was less than the volatility of the low-grade bond index. Once one controls for these differences in duration, the standard deviation of the low-grade bond index is greater than the standard deviation volatility of the high-grade bonds indexes.[12]

Estimation Errors in Expected Returns and Volatility

The relative rankings of the compounded rates of return of low-grade bonds relative to governments, corporates, the S&P 500, and small stocks varied substantially from one subperiod to another. In contrast, the rankings of the standard deviations of monthly returns were much more stable across subperiods. This result is exactly what one would expect. Merton (1980) showed that the accuracy of an estimate of volatility of a stationary return process[13] depends upon the number of subintervals within any specific period of time, whereas the accuracy of an estimate of the expected compounded rate of return depends on the overall length of the estimation period, not the number of subintervals.

As an example, if a researcher has an estimation period of ten years, the estimate of volatility will be more accurate the greater the number of subintervals in these ten years. Monthly returns will provide

---

[11] See Blume, Keim and Patel (1991).

[12] In making this adjustment, the call features of the low-grade bonds turned out to have more of an impact than the adjustment for the coupon levels, despite the fact that the adjustment for call features was not complete. In fact, we were able to account only for the volatility of interest rates in valuing the call provisions of each low-grade bond and only up to the end of the call protection period. We ignored the value of the call after the call protection period, the increased possibility of early call because of credit improvement or balance sheet restructuring, and the possibility of default. With these further adjustments, the gap would have been even greater.

[13] His proof assumed a stationary diffusion process, a commonly used process to describe security returns.

more accurate estimates of volatility than yearly returns, and weekly returns will provide more accurate estimates of volatility than monthly returns. In contrast, there is no increase in the accuracy of an estimate of the expected compound rate of return by increasing the number of subperiods. The only way to increase the accuracy of this estimate is to increase the length of the estimation period.

Figure 2 contains a heuristic demonstration of this argument using returns from two hypothetical investments. The solid line represents an investment that grows at a steady pace---in this case, 10 percent per year. The dashed line represents a much more volatile investment. On the assumption that the returns for each of these investments are drawn from stationary processes, an investor could reliably determine that the investment portrayed by the dashed line is the more volatile investment. Yet, an investor would be at a loss to determine from the data in Figure 2 which investment has the greatest expected compound rate of growth.

3. The Covariability of Asset Categories

The purpose of this section is analyze the covariability of the returns of low-grade bonds with the returns of other asset categories. The main conclusion is that low-grade bonds display characteristics of both stocks and bonds. Moreover, the relative importance of the returns of stocks and bonds in explaining the returns of low-grade bonds changes over time.

For the entire fourteen and a half years from 1977 through June 1991, the correlation of low-grade bonds with government bonds is 0.62 and with small stocks is 0.54 (Table 3). In contrast, the correlation of high-grade corporate bonds with governments is 0.95 and with small stocks is 0.20. Thus, in terms of correlation coefficients, low-grade bonds have more equity characteristics and less pure bond characteristics than high-grade corporate bonds.

Although low-grade bonds have both the characteristics of bonds and equities, the importance of these two markets in explaining the returns on the low-grade bond index varies over time. An examination of the seven successive two-year periods from July 1977 through June 1991 shows that there is substantial variability in the correlation coefficients of low-grade bonds with government bonds and small stocks (Figure 3). Over these seven two-year periods, the correlation of low-grade bonds with governments varies from 0.22 to 0.81, and with small

FIGURE 2

Estimating Expected Returns and Standard Deviation

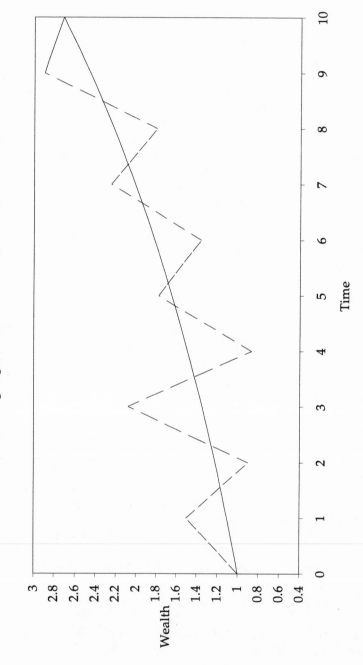

TABLE 3

**Correlations of Monthly Returns for Various Asset Classes
January 1977 - June 1991**

	Long-Term High-Grade Corporate Bonds	Long-Term Low-Grade Bonds	S&P 500	Small Stocks
Long-Term Government Bonds	0.95	0.62	0.37	0.20
Long-Term High-Grade Corporate Bonds		0.69	0.34	0.20
Long-Term Low-Grade Bonds			0.52	0.54
S&P 500				0.81

Source: These statistics are based upon several indexes of monthly returns. From 1977 through 1988, the bonds underlying the low-grade bond index are all non-convertible with face value at time of issue of greater than $25 million and with time to maturity of at least ten years from the date on which any return is calculated. The returns for the individual bonds from 1982 through 1988 are based upon bid prices from Drexel Burnham Lambert and Salomon Brothers and prior to 1982 upon prices from the *S&P Bond Guide*. The return indexes from 1977 through 1988 are averages of these returns by month. For 1989, Drexel calculated a monthly return index using bid prices in virtually the same way as the 1977-1988 indexes were calculated, and this index was used to extend the sample through 1989. The returns from January 1990 through June 1991 are derived from the Salomon Brothers long-term bond index for low-grade bonds. The returns for (1) the S&P 500, (2) a value-weighted portfolio of common stocks in the smallest size quintile on the NYSE, (3) the Salomon Brothers index of long-term high-grade (rated A and above) corporate bonds, and (4) long-term (approximately twenty years to maturity) government bonds are from Ibbotson Associates.

FIGURE 3
Correlations of Low-Grade Bonds
With Treasury Bonds and Small Stocks

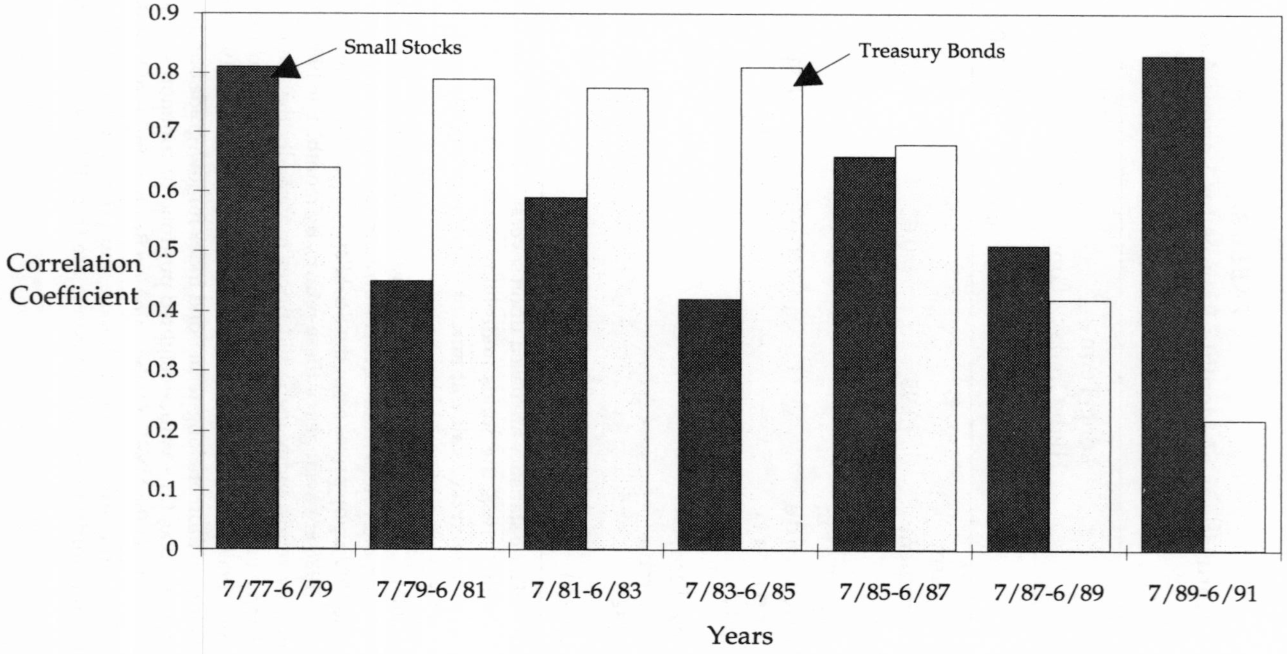

stocks from 0.42 to 0.83. In three of the two-year periods, the returns of low-grade bonds are more highly correlated with the returns of small stocks than with the returns of governments, and in the other four periods, the reverse occurs. The most recent two-year period ending June 1991 saw the greatest correlation between low-grade bonds and small stocks (0.83) and the smallest correlation between low-grade bonds and government bonds (0.22).

To explore the simultaneous relation between low-grade bonds and other asset categories, we ran regressions of monthly returns of low-grade bonds on the returns of long-term governments and small stocks. Previous research has found that the returns on small stocks and low-grade bonds in January exceed on average the returns of higher quality bonds and larger stocks. To incorporate such a January effect, we added a dummy variable assuming a value of 1 for January to some of the regressions. In the regression for the overall period with the January dummy variable excluded, the coefficient on governments is 0.43 and on small stocks is 0.22 with an adjusted R-squared of 0.57. The inclusion of the January dummy has little effect on these coefficients and leads to a modest increase in the R-squared to 0.58. Nonetheless, the coefficient of the January dummy is positive and significant. Since the returns of small firms already contain a January effect, one might have expected the coefficient of the January dummy to be zero. The fact that it is not zero indicates that the January effect for low-grade bonds may be of a slightly different magnitude from the January effect in the returns of small firms.

To examine the stationarity of these regressions, we reran the regressions for each of the seven two-year periods ending in June 1991. For the first six periods from July 1977 through June 1989, the estimated coefficients on governments and small stocks are quite stationary with the coefficients ranging from 0.22 to 0.46 for governments and from 0.07 to 0.22 for small stocks (Table 4). The table only includes the regressions with the January dummy. Like the overall period, dropping the January dummy had little effect on the estimated coefficients or the R-squared's.

Consistent with the previous analyses of correlations, the estimated coefficients in the last subperiod from July 1989 through June 1991 are quite different from the earlier years. The coefficient on long-term governments is -0.24 and not significant, while the coefficient on small stocks is 0.60. Thus, in the last two years, low-grade returns are more sensitive to small stocks than previously. A plot of the major market indexes for these two years shows the close relation between small stocks and low-grade bonds (Figure 4). During the six months from

TABLE 4
Regressions of Low-Grade Bond Returns on Bond and Stock Market Returns for Various Dates

Dates	Intercept	January Dummy	Long-Term Governments	Small Stocks	R^2
1/1977 - 6/1991	0.18 (1.22)	-	0.43 (10.63)	0.22 (8.46)	0.57
	0.10 (0.65)	1.05 (2.03)	0.44 (10.87)	0.21 (8.07)	0.58
7/1977 - 6/1979	-0.21 (-0.91)	0.87 (1.11)	0.38 (2.19)	0.18 (5.00)	0.72
7/1979 - 6/1981	-0.51 (-0.86)	2.74 (1.53)	0.66 (6.52)	0.20 (2.08)	0.71
7/1981 - 6/1983	0.43 (0.92)	1.51 (1.02)	0.46 (4.87)	0.22 (2.53)	0.67
7/1983 - 6/1985	0.37 (1.51)	1.75 (1.97)	0.44 (6.46)	0.07 (1.24)	0.72
7/1985 - 6/1987	0.43 (1.62)	0.98 (1.06)	0.22 (3.04)	0.15 (2.05)	0.56
7/1987 - 6/1989	0.41 (1.47)	0.45 (0.43)	0.33 (3.25)	0.16 (3.95)	0.51
7/1989 - 6/1991	0.59 (1.13)	-0.44 (-0.25)	-0.24 (-0.95)	0.60 (6.59)	0.66

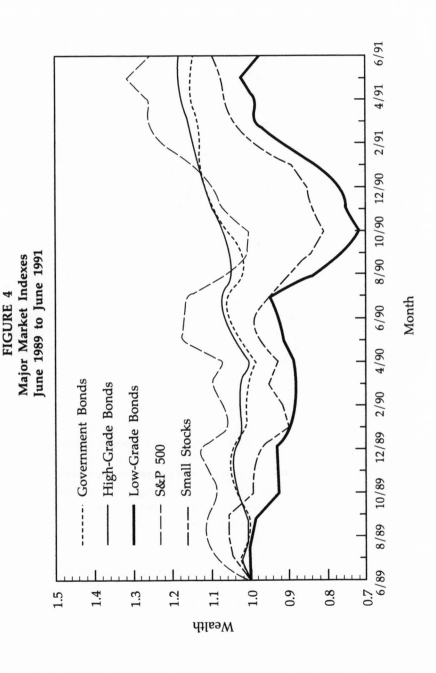

FIGURE 4
Major Market Indexes
June 1989 to June 1991

.... Government Bonds

——— High-Grade Bonds

━━━ Low-Grade Bonds

– – – S&P 500

— — Small Stocks

Wealth

Month

June 1989 through December 1989, there were substantial declines in the values of both of these indexes, while S&P stocks and the higher grade index experienced gains. For the next six months, the five asset groups moved very much in parallel. This parallel movement is clearer if the plot of the indexes begins in December 1989 (Figure 5).

From July 1990 through October 1990, there was a wide divergence in the movement of stocks, low-grade bonds, and the higher grade bonds. Small stocks declined the most. The decline in both S&P stocks and low-grade bonds was about the same. The higher grade bonds experienced some decline and then a recovery. Following October 1990, stocks and low-grade bonds experience substantial recoveries through the June 1991. As already mentioned, one would expect low-grade bonds to realize losses when small stocks do poorly and vice versa, but the swings should not be as great. An analysis not reported here shows that the losses on low-grade bonds, and their subsequent recovery, were greater than their historical relation to small stocks would predict.

A question this study cannot answer is whether the behavior of the low-grade market in the last two years represents a permanent change in the behavior of long-term low-grade bonds or a temporary aberration. In this regard, it is in-teresting that the correlation between low-grade bonds and small stocks is almost as great in the two years ending June 1979 as it is in the most recent two years.

4. Some Implications for Insurance Portfolios

In 1952, Nobel laureate Harry Markowitz developed a formal theory of diversification. The essence of this theory is that investors should focus their attention on the returns of the entire portfolio---not specifically on the individual assets. Of course, individual assets are important, but their importance stems from how their returns interact with each other. If the returns of two assets are not perfectly positively or negatively correlated, a properly weighted portfolio will experience no more risk or volatility, and less risk except in one special case, than the volatility of either asset held by itself.

This paper establishes that the correlation of the returns of low-grade bonds and other financial assets, including long-term governments and equities, is not perfect--implying that low-grade bonds have a place in any well-diversified portfolio. To say that they should be in a portfolio does not necessarily mean that they should be held long. If an asset is sufficiently overpriced in comparison to other assets, portfolio

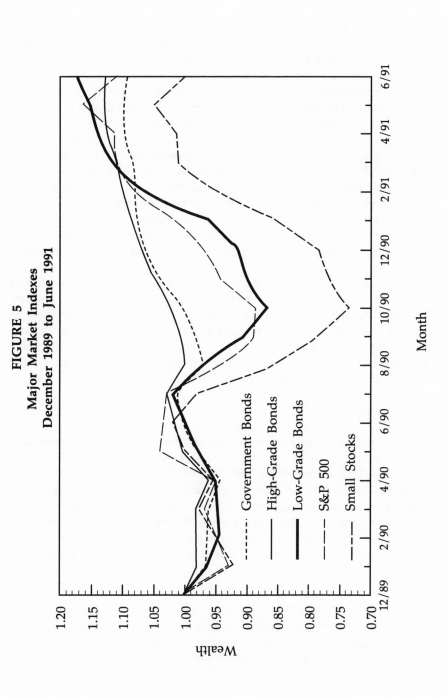

FIGURE 5
Major Market Indexes
December 1989 to June 1991

Government Bonds
High-Grade Bonds
Low-Grade Bonds
S&P 500
Small Stocks

Wealth

Month

theory might call for a short position in that asset. However, the results of this paper and other papers that we have coauthored suggest that low-grade bonds are not grossly mispriced--either too low or too high. In this case, a positive position is warranted.

In investing in low-grade bonds, it is important to recognize that these bonds do default and that a portion of the high coupon is really a return of principal in anticipation of a possible default. Consequently, treating the full coupon as income overstates the true income of these bonds. The easiest way to adjust for this overstatement is to carry low-grade bonds at market value. If a bond becomes more likely to default, its price will fall, and this loss will reduce the coupon payment.[14] A less satisfactory approach is to set up a reserve for potential losses or to use some adjusted book value of the bond. Either of these accounting adjustments will work if the adjustments exactly mirror market losses. If not, the financial health of an insurance company will be incorrectly stated.

Indeed, there is a strong argument to be made that all assets and liabilities of an insurance company should be carried at market. Historically, it was difficult to value the often complex liabilities at market, but our new understanding of the pricing of derivative claims promises to simplify this task. Thus, a direct measure of the health of an insurance company is the difference between the market value of the assets and the market value of the liabilities.

5. Conclusion

This paper updates the authors' earlier analyses of long-term low-grade bonds. The volatility of low-grade bonds has increased in the last two years, and during these last two years, low-grade bonds tracked small stocks more closely than they have historically. Even with this increase in volatility, the volatility of low-grade bonds is still not that much different from higher grade long-term bonds. The evidence indicates that, even in this most recent period, the volatility of returns of low-grade bonds is considerably less than that of common stocks.

---

[14] Of course, the market value of these fixed-income obligations, as well as any long-term fixed-income obligation, like home mortgages, will also fluctuate in response to movements in the general level of interest rates.

REFERENCES

Altman, E. I., 1987, "The anatomy of the high-yield bond market", *Financial Analysts Journal*, July-August, 12-25.

Altman, E. I., 1989, "Measuring corporate bond mortality and performance", *Journal of Finance*, 44, 909-922.

Asquith, P., D. W. Mullins, Jr., and E. D. Wolff, 1989, "Original issue high-yield bonds: Aging analysis of defaults, exchanges and calls," *Journal of Finance*, 44, 923-952.

Blume, M. E. and D. B. Keim, 1987, "Lower-grade bonds: Their risks and returns," *Financial Analysts Journal*, July-August, 26-33.

Blume, M. E. and D. B. Keim, 1991, "Risks and returns of low-grade bonds: An update," *Financial Analysts Journal*, September-October, 85-89.

Blume, M. E., D. B. Keim and S. Patel, 1991, "Returns and volatility of low-grade bonds: 1977-1989," *Journal of Finance*, 46, 49-74.

Merton, R. C., 1980, "On estimating the expected return on the market: An exploratory investigation," *Journal of Financial Economics*, 8, 323-362.

5 THE PARADOX OF PERFORMANCE MEASUREMENT

William H. Panning
Vice President
Investment Division
ITT Hartford

The ideas and opinions expressed in this paper are those of the author's, and do not necessarily reflect the policies, practices, or opinions of ITT Hartford, its subsidiaries and affiliates, or its management. I am grateful to the numerous colleagues whose patient listening, stimulating questions, and insightful comments helped to shape what I have written.

Portfolio management is investment engineering.
-- Charles D. Ellis, *Investment Policy* (1985)

. . . engineering design has as its first and foremost
objective the obviation of failure.
-- Henry Petroski, *To Engineer is Human:
The Role of Failure in Successful Design*
(1985)

. . . portfolio management is primarily a *defensive*
process. . .   The basic responsibility of portfolio
managers . . . is to control and manage risk.
-- Charles D. Ellis, *Investment Policy* (1985)

. . . it is as much the designer's business to know how
any structure might fail as it is a chess player's to
know how one false move may lead to checkmate.
-- Henry Petroski, *To Engineer is Human:
The Role of Failure in Successful Design*
(1985)

I vividly remember my introduction to the insurance business. After nearly a decade of teaching and research at several universities -- part of it here at the Wharton School -- I found the world of insurance both fascinating and, at times, puzzling. My first surprise was the discovery that, despite the enormous quantities of memos and reports that it both produces and consumes, the insurance business is fundamentally an oral culture. Unlike academe, where one typically learns from books and journals, in the insurance firms with which I am familiar the things that matter most are hardly ever written down. To find out why something is done one way rather than another, one cannot simply consult a memo or report. One has to ask someone. Fortunately, a newcomer can ask all sorts of questions without being thought stupid. So I did. Thanks to patient and knowledgeable colleagues, I learned more and more about this fascinating and complex business we are in.

As I learned, and my questions became more sophisticated, I discovered that some questions were puzzling not only to me but also, it turned out, to others as well. This was really exciting, because in the academic world from which I had come, puzzling questions are the stimulus for scientific or technological progress. I began to suspect -- and have since become convinced -- that in the business world, these puzzles really indicate potential opportunities for improving what we do and thereby increasing profitability, customer satisfaction, or shareholder value. My objective here is to persuade you that this is so for one such puzzle: how to measure fixed-income investment performance.

Briefly, my argument is this. First, measuring investment performance is important to insurers -- or should be -- because they and their environment have changed in three critical ways: (a) thanks to increased competition, their profit margins have eroded, so that investment success is more critical; (b) both their products and the investments that fund them have become more complex and more tightly linked to one another, so that successful investment is more difficult; and (c) investment markets have become more volatile, so that problems can arise more quickly and become more serious. Second, the performance measures often used in fixed-income investing have serious limitations, the most important of which is their insensitivity to variations in risk. A potential -- and sometime actual -- consequence of their use is to encourage, rather than control, risk-taking, and therefore to create the *paradox of performance measurement:* what appear by our measurements to be "good" decisions may actually harm policyholders and shareholders by reducing the value of the firm. Third, this trap can be avoided by changing the focus of evaluation to encompass the future as well as the past, and the risks incurred as well as the results achieved. Fortunately, the very changes that have made performance measurement more important have also brought into existence the concepts and tools needed to implement this change in focus. The challenge we face is to adapt and use them.

I'll present this argument by addressing four questions in turn: (1) Why should investment performance matter to insurers? (2) How is it typically done? (3) What are the pitfalls in current practice? (4) How can we avoid them?

Why Measure Investment Performance?

Suppose for a moment that, like Rip Van Winkle, a portfolio manager for a life insurance company fell asleep in 1970 and woke today. Imagine some of the dramatic changes he would perceive in the industry and in its environment. First, he would discover that profit margins in the industry have become thinner, that new products have become more complex, and that sales growth and profitability are more tightly coupled to investment performance than ever before. Second, he would perceive that investment markets have also become vastly more complex. He would be astonished at the tremendous growth of mortgage-backed securities, junk bonds, and options markets, and intrigued by the intricacies of collateralized mortgage obligations (CMO's) and other derivative securities. Third, he would certainly be astounded by the magnitude and rapidity of changes in market yields and prices. He would discover that the stock market can now lose a fourth of its value in a single day, that Treasury yields can move by 500 basis points in a month or two, and that in response to mergers or buyouts bonds can shift in credit quality from AA to BB or lower in a matter of days or weeks. In other words, he would learn that fixed-income assets can lose their economic value more easily, more quickly, and in more complicated ways, and that maintaining profitability has become more difficult and requires far more sophistication. Clearly, the need to monitor and control investment performance has become substantially greater.

There are some sobering analogies between these recent changes in our industry and environment -- increased complexity of both assets and liabilities, tighter coupling between them, and increased market volatility -- and historical changes that have occurred in the world of industry. As Perrow (1984, pp. 11-12) points out,

>Human-made catastrophes appear to have increased with
>industrialization as we built devices that could crash,
>sink, burn, or explode. In the last fifty years, however,
>and particularly in the last twenty-five, to the usual
>cause of accidents -- some component failure, which
>could be prevented in the future -- was added a new
>cause: interactive complexity in the presence of tight
>coupling, producing a system accident. . . The systems
>have become more complicated because either they are
>dealing with more deadly substances, or we demand
>they function in ever more hostile environments or with
>ever greater speed and volume.

Perrow presents compelling evidence that industrial systems with greater
complexity or tighter coupling between components or processes are
more prone to have accidents. Systems that exhibit both these key
characteristics include nuclear power plants, chemical plants, space
missions, and large aircraft.

My point is not that our industry has increased in complexity or
tight coupling of components (assets and liabilities) and processes
(investment and sales) to such extent that it closely resembles any of the
high-technology systems just mentioned. Rather, I am arguing only that
we have moved, and are still moving, in that direction. As suggestive
evidence consider the enormous loss sustained by a major Wall Street
firm that first mispriced and then subsequently failed to properly hedge
a somewhat complex security it had created, the FSLIC takeover of a
multibillion dollar savings and loan after its complex hedges of mortgage-
backed securities and derivatives failed to perform as anticipated, the
recent liquidity crisis at Mutual Benefit Life as policyholders exercised
options that once seemed innocuous, the earlier demise of First Executive
after the unanticipated precipitous decline in the junk bond market, and
the present concern of policyholders, regulators, and rating agencies with
the possibility of more such "accidents."

Now I hasten to assert my firm belief that our industry
is financially sound, and that much of the public and regulatory hand
wringing is unwarranted. For the purpose at hand, however, I hope that
we can temporarily set aside the necessarily defensive posture into which
we have recently been thrust, and consider the possibility that our
industry has indeed changed in crucial ways that deserve our attention.
The evolution of industrial systems that exhibit complexity and tight

TABLE 1
Some Common Measures of Investment Performance

Performance Measure:	New Investment Yield	Portfolio Book Yield	Portfolio Book Income	Portfolio Total Return (RCY)
Marginal vs. Total	Marginal	Total	Total	Total
Accounting vs. Economic	Accounting	Accounting	Accounting	Economic
Stability over Time	Low	High	High	Low
Ease of Calculation	High	High	High	Medium
Sensitivity to Changes in Credit Quality	None	Partial	Partial	Total
Sensitivity to Changes in Interest-Rates	None	Partial	Partial	Total

coupling required corresponding changes in the way in which they were managed. If, as I have suggested, our own industry has moved in that direction, then it may be appropriate to inquire whether similar changes are needed in the way we manage our own business. As one small part of this broader inquiry, let us examine how investment performance is measured in practice.

How is Fixed-Income Performance Typically Measured?

Fixed-income performance measurement consists of two simple steps: (1) some measure of portfolio performance is calculated; (2) this measure is compared to some index or reference number. Let me briefly review some of the most common ways in which this is done.[1]

(1) What performance measure should be calculated?

Table 1 describes four measures of fixed-income investment performance commonly used by life insurers. The first two are weighted (by book value) average yields on securities. However, *new investment yield* encompasses only securities purchased during the measurement period, whereas *portfolio book yield* reflects the yields both on new purchases and also on securities already held in the portfolio.[2] The first

---

[1] I will focus specifically upon fixed-income performance measurement as it is typically practiced by insurers. For more general reviews of performance measurement see Dietz and Kirschman (1983) and Williams (1983).

[2] *New investment yield* is the value-weighted average yield of new purchases during a period. The yield of a security is the internal rate of return of its future cash flows, given its price. The standard methods for calculating yields for different types of securities are described in Lynch and Mayle (1986). *Portfolio book yield* is the book-value-weighted average book yield of its component securities. *Portfolio book income* is the total accounting income generated by an investment portfolio during a specified period. Because book values, yields, and income are numbers generated for accounting purposes, their computation is governed by rules established by the Financial Accounting Standard Board (FASB) and its predecessor, the Accounting Principles Board (APB), in various opinions and bulletins. On the

thus reflects the marginal impact of purchase decisions made during the measurement period, while the second incorporates the effect during the measurement period of decisions made in preceding periods. Although portfolio book yield reflects decisions to sell securities and purchase new ones, opportunities to do so may be limited by the presence in the portfolio of less liquid securities, by constraints on the magnitude of capital gains and losses triggered by turnover, or by a reasonable desire to minimize transaction costs. When portfolio turnover is low, new investment yield will fluctuate with changes in interest rates and credit spreads, whereas portfolio book yield will typically exhibit much greater stability over time. Because both measures are defined by accounting rules rather than by external price measures, they are easy to calculate.

As its name suggests, *portfolio book income* reflects the total investment income actually generated by a portfolio during the measurement period. It is therefore affected by both the magnitude and timing of cash inflows and outflows during the period -- variables typically outside the control of the portfolio manager. Portfolio book income therefore reflects more than just investment performance. If

---

date of purchase, a security's book value and yield are identical to its market value and yield (or "trade" yield). For a security with fixed cash flows purchased at par, its book value, book yield, and book income will remain constant until it matures or is sold, unless the receipt of those cash flows becomes sufficiently doubtful that the security is considered "impaired" and must be written down to a lower value. For securities purchased at a premium or discount, the book yield remains constant but the book value is adjusted throughout its life to converge to par value at its maturity. Book income for a given period is equal to accrued interest on the security during that period adjusted to reflect any change during that period in its book value (amortization of premium or accrual of discount). Unfortunately, the accounting rules governing the calculation of book values and yields create anomalies due to the fact that interest accrues linearly and coupon payments are not spaced evenly over time. As a consequence, the book value and income of a bond purchased at par can in fact fluctuate slightly over time unless special adjustments are made in the computational algorithm. Applications of the accounting rules to securities whose cash flows can vary (as with mortgage-backed or other asset-backed securities subject to prepayments) involve far greater complexities that have been the subject of recent FASB opinions.

adjustments are made to remove this sensitivity to cash inflows and outflows, the resulting modified measures closely resemble portfolio book yield. The sole advantage of portfolio book income is that it can easily be compared to a business plan.

Unlike yield measures, which reflect only investment income, *portfolio total return* (sometimes called realized compound yield, or RCY) includes both investment income and changes in the market value of the portfolio during the measurement period. Ideally, total return should be calculated daily, and then compounded over the measurement period, to render it insensitive to the magnitude and timing of cash inflows and outflows.[3] Because it incorporates market prices, total return

---

[3] For a given measurement period, *total return* for a security or unchanging portfolio is [change in market price plus change in accrued interest plus cash interest received]/[beginning market price plus accrued interest]. For a portfolio for which cash has not been added or withdrawn during the period (except for receipt of cash interest payments), an equivalent definition is [ending market price plus accrued interest]/[beginning market price plus accrued interest] -1. When total returns on a portfolio or security are compared over different periods of unequal length, or for periods longer than a year, the appropriate measure is *annualized* total return, which is $[1+\text{total return for the period}]^{365/d}$ -1, where d is the number of days in the period. Total returns calculated separately for multiple shorter periods (days, weeks, or months) can be compounded to give a total return for a longer period. Total return for the longer period is equal to $[1+tr_1] \times [1+tr_2] \times \ldots \times [1+tr_n]$ -1, where tr_1 is the total return in the first subperiod, and so on. Total return measures can be distorted when deposits or withdrawals are made during the measurement period. To see why this is so, consider two portfolio managers who hold *the same securities in identical proportions* for three months in which returns are 0%, 10%, and 0%, respectively. Manager A begins with $100 and three months later has $110, for a total return of 10%. Manager B likewise begins with $100, but $100 is added to his portfolio at the end of the first month and withdrawn at the end of the second month. At the end of three months he has $120, but the additional $10 reflects only the effect of fortuitous deposits and withdrawals. The correct measure of quarterly total return in this case is not 120/100 - 1, but rather 100/100 x 220/200 x 120/120 - 1, or 10%. As this example shows, deposits or withdrawals must be reflected in both the numerator and denominator of the total return calculation. The frequent and unpredictable nature of deposits and withdrawals, together with the advent of computer technology, has made

reflects the real economic change in the value of the portfolio, which may deviate substantially from the change in its accounting or book value. This link to market prices makes total return both more volatile than accounting measures of return, and also more difficult to calculate, especially for portfolios with substantial proportions of private placements, commercial mortgages, and real estate, for which market values must often be estimated rather than simply observed.

These four measures also differ in their sensitivity to credit risk and interest-rate risk. New investment yield is sensitive to neither, since it reflects only *promised* future income. Portfolio book yield and book income are partially sensitive to credit risk, since they incorporate the effect (write downs and non-admitted income) of defaults among securities already held in the portfolio. However, so long as securities do not default, mere deterioration in their credit quality will not affect these measures (unless the receipt of promised future cash flows from a security becomes improbable, so that a write down is triggered). These two measures can be sensitive to changes in interest rates, but only to the extent that the portfolio includes securities for which the magnitude or timing of interest income depends on rate levels (e.g., mortgage pass-throughs, some mortgage-backed derivatives, variable-rate securities, and bonds that are called during the measurement period).

Total return, by contrast, is sensitive to changes in both credit quality and interest-rates as they are reflected in security prices. A deterioration in credit quality, for example, will normally be reflected in a lower price, and therefore in a lower total return, even if the security does not default. Similarly, the price of a security will reflect not only changes in market rates but also changes in the magnitude and timing of its expected future cash flows. Consider, for example, two 10% bonds purchased at par, one of them callable in a year, the other noncallable. If yields fall substantially, the price of the callable bond will rise by less than the price of the noncallable bond, due to the now-increased likelihood of its being called. Total return will therefore be lower for the callable bond than for the noncallable one. By contrast, the book yields and book income for the two will be identical, unaffected by the change in rates and in expected future cash flows. The book yield or income for a portfolio with callable bonds will change only if bonds do in fact call

---

daily calculation of total return a *de facto* industry standard.

during the measurement period and therefore have to be replaced with lower-yielding substitutes.

In practice, a particular measure or combination of measures is chosen that reflects the type of product that the portfolio is funding and the constraints under which the portfolio manager must operate. For example, new investment yield is often used when product sales depend heavily upon promised yield, or when the portfolio consists largely of illiquid securities. On the other hand, total return is typically employed for portfolios that are actively managed.

(2) To what should the performance measure be compared?

Investment performance is relative rather than absolute: it has to be compared to some value consisting of (a) competitor performance, (b) a market-based index, or (c) a customized liability index.

Our understandable desire to compare investment performance to that of our principal competitors is, in practice, inversely proportional to our ability to do so. The difficulty is that public sources of information concerning competitors' portfolios lack both the focus and precision needed for such comparisons. Although book income is reported, and approximate book yields and new commitment yields can be calculated from available data, these measures are typically not reported or calculable by product line. Moreover, differences between one's own performance and that of competitors may be due to a different mix of business, differences in the volume and timing of cash flows, or differences in risk tolerance. Consequently, although estimates of competitor performance are frequently examined, they can seldom be relied upon as a definitive basis for comparison.

When asked what inferences about God might be drawn from the study of nature, the biologist J. B. S. Haldane replied, "I'm really not sure, except that He must be inordinately fond of beetles." There are, it seems, more than 300,000 species of beetles. During the past two decades, fixed-income indices have become the beetles of the investment world. Each index describes the performance over a specified measurement period of hypothetical portfolios consisting of particular categories of securities.[4]

---

[4] For a partial list of available indices see Williams and Conwell (1983). For details concerning index construction see Merrill Lynch (1985).

Indices are distinguished from one another by the particular subset of securities that they include, as defined by (a) security type (e.g., Treasuries, corporates, mortgage-backed, dollar-denominated foreign securities, and so on), (b) the maximum and minimum maturity, (c) maximum and minimum credit quality, and (d) minimum par amount outstanding. For example, the Salomon Brothers Long-Term High-Grade Index consists of domestic corporate bonds with a minimum maturity of twelve years, a minimum quality of AA, and minimum outstanding par amount of $25 million. Given the enormous variety of fixed-income securities in existence, additional detailed specifications are often required to determine eligibility for inclusion in a particular index. For example, flower bonds (specially-designated Treasury securities that can be used to pay inheritance taxes) are typically excluded from indices, as are floating rate securities, equipment trust certificates, and convertible bonds.

Comparing investment performance to an index is complicated by the fact that the index numbers provided by different firms may differ even though they are apparently based on the same set of component securities for the same measurement period. There are several reasons for this. (1) There may be slight differences in the set of securities included. (2) The selection of securities may occur at different times. Some firms identify the securities to be included at the beginning of the period, other firms do so at the end of the period. A bond that qualifies for inclusion at the beginning of a month may not qualify at the end, due to a change in its maturity or credit quality. (3) Because there is no central exchange for most fixed-income securities, the same bond may be priced differently by different firms. For example, although traders provide the prices of some bonds included in the index, the prices of other bonds will be estimated by methods that may differ slightly among firms. Moreover, traders at different firms may themselves differ in their end-of-day price estimates for bonds that trade infrequently. Also, if new bonds are issued that are eligible for inclusion in the index, firms may differ in whether they use bid prices (as for the other bonds) or ask prices, which reflect the transaction cost of purchasing the security for a real portfolio. (4) Firms may differ in their assumptions about the treatment of coupon income received during the period. For example, some firms assume that the coupons remain as cash until they are reinvested on the next index calculation date, whereas other firms assume that intraperiod cash flows are invested at the average one-month Treasury Bill rate. (5) Firms may differ in the frequency with which they calculate index returns. Some do so daily, others monthly. Index returns calculated for a whole month may differ from returns calculated daily and then compounded to obtain a monthly value, due to the resulting differences in the frequency of assumed reinvestment.

Selecting an index to which a portfolio's performance can be compared is often difficult for several reasons. (1) The securities included in any index are arbitrary, and do not necessarily reflect the market opportunities typically available to a portfolio manager. For example, many of the securities included in broad-based indices seldom trade, and although their aggregate weight in the index may be small, they do influence its performance. (2) A portfolio manager may be limited by constraints not reflected in an index, particularly one that is limited to a small subset of securities. Suppose, for example, that the index selected for comparison is limited to securities with maturities between five and seven years. Over time, securities that were initially included in this index will disappear from it as their maturities fall below five years, and others will be added as their initially longer maturities decrease to seven years. These changes in composition -- in effect, purchases and sales from this hypothetical portfolio -- are all reflected in the index at the bid price. A real portfolio with identical purchases and sales would in fact incur transaction costs, as its manager may be unwilling or unable to purchase or sell securities due to tax considerations, constraints on capital gains or losses, or lack of ready cash. Moreover, prudence typically dictates the need to maintain a diversified portfolio, whereas the securities in an index may be highly concentrated in a few sectors or firms. (3) Finally, as distinct from a mutual fund, the purpose of an insurance portfolio is to fund liabilities of some sort, which no readily available index is likely to adequately resemble. This limitation is the most serious of all, for investment decisions that outperform an ill-chosen index may in fact decrease the profitability or net worth of an insurer.

Concern that this may occur has stimulated the development of customized indices that can be tailored to more closely resemble insurer liabilities. In its simplest form a customized index is simply a weighted average of numerous existing but narrowly-defined indices, selected and weighted to resemble the cash flows or duration (a measure of price sensitivity to changes in interest rates) of the liabilities being funded. In its most refined form a customized liability index is constructed by selecting individual securities from a large database and appropriately weighting each of them (Babbel, Stricker, and Vanderhoof, 1990). A key decision in constructing such an index is the credit quality distribution of the securities selected, which should closely resemble the credit quality of the securities that are appropriate for the actual portfolio. Because customized indices are developed by specific Wall Street firms to reflect the unique liabilities of individual clients, they can exhibit considerable variety, so that generalizations concerning them are difficult and potentially misleading.

What are the Pitfalls in Performance Measurement?

Let's say that the measurement period has ended, the performance numbers and the index or competitor numbers to which they will be compared have all been gathered, and we await the result. The situation reminds one of Gertrude Stein, an author and something of a cult figure, as she lay on her deathbed, surrounded by friends and disciples hoping to hear some final and definitive words of wisdom. When her silence had become almost unbearable, one of them learned forward and whispered, "Gertrude, what is the answer?" Opening her eyes, Stein responded, "What is the question?"

Suppose the performance measure exceeded some comparison number by, say, 100 basis points. What question does that answer? Does it, as commonly supposed, tell us how well the portfolio manager has performed? There are sound reasons for believing it does not: (a) measurement error, and (b) random effects.

By *measurement error* I mean that the numbers we obtain may only imperfectly reflect the true state of affairs. In his book *Down and Out in Paris and London*, the British essayist George Orwell recounts his experiences in those cities as a dishwasher in several fine hotels and restaurants. In almost nauseous detail he describes the horrifying conditions in which the gourmet dishes so admired by patrons were in fact prepared. In a similar way, the crisply printed performance numbers we see and rely on often conceal their imprecision.

Of the performance measures described earlier, total return is the most susceptible to measurement error, since it depends upon market prices. Although securities that are common, highly liquid, and frequently traded can be priced rather precisely (that is, prices obtained from different sources would be nearly identical), securities that lack these characteristics cannot. The latter category would include most private placements, commercial mortgages, real estate, CMO's, and other derivatives, at least some of which are held in the portfolios of many insurers. The commercial services that price such securities do so by estimating their prices from those of similar but frequently traded securities for which real market prices are available.[5] Unfortunately, the prices obtained from different services often disagree -- sometimes substantially. In one instance with which I am familiar, a billion dollar portfolio was priced by two different services. The difference between the total return measures calculated from the two sets of prices exceeded the difference between our criteria for average and maximum performance!

A recent study by Reese and Guy (1990) found that although error in estimating total return decreases with the size of the portfolio, the reduction is typically not as large as one might anticipate, since the market value of large portfolios is often concentrated in a relatively small number of holdings. Moreover, since prices must be calculated at both the beginning and end of the measurement period, the potential error is in fact doubled, since pricing errors are nearly (but not quite) random over time. They conclude that for most fixed income portfolios, imprecision in measuring total return is likely to be anywhere from 14 to 70 basis points annually. Increasing the length of the measurement period reduces this error by the square root of the number of years included. For example, lengthening the period to four years would reduce error by half.

But this is only part the story. Since we are comparing this estimate of portfolio total return to an index that also exhibits measurement error, the margin of error in the difference between the two may be even larger (not doubled, however, since the portfolio and the

---

[5] The market values of private securities are estimated from the prices of similar but publicly-traded securities issued by the same firm (or, if there are none, by another firm in the same industry) and then adjusted for differences in coupon, maturity, credit quality, and liquidity. Valuing real estate and commercial mortgages is far more difficult, since the relevant properties are always unique (if only by virtue of differences in location -- but location has substantial effect on their value). In principle, valuation should be based on an appraisal, but full-blown appraisals are expensive and therefore infrequent. In practice, at some firms periodic appraisals are performed and supplemented by more frequent but less thorough property reviews to provide interim values. At other firms, these investments are simply carried at book value, which is then utilized in calculating portfolio total return.

index presumably contain some of the same securities, and since pricing errors tend to be correlated across securities).

These difficulties in satisfactorily measuring total return create a strong temptation to adopt one of the other three measures described earlier, since book income and yield can at least be calculated accurately. Unfortunately, these measures have other characteristics that limit their usefulness in assessing investment performance. Consider, for example, two hypothetical portfolio managers who purchased and held identical amounts of AAA-rated securities with identical yields, so that at year-end new investment yield, portfolio book yield, and portfolio book income were the same for both portfolios. These measures would therefore fail to reflect the fact that the securities in one portfolio remained AAA while those in the other declined to BBB. Total return, by contrast, would reflect the difference, for it includes not only the income generated by each portfolio but also any price changes triggered by changes in credit quality. Error, like sin, can occur through omission as well as commission.

Even if measurement error were totally absent, attempts to quantify investment skill are hindered by the presence of *random effects*. Our own experiences in the classroom or in sports should remind us how often, as Koheleth the preacher so elegantly puts it in *Ecclesiastes*, "the race is not to the swift, nor the battle to the strong, nor bread to the wise, nor riches to the intelligent, nor favor to the men of skill; but time and chance happen to them all." (In speaking of those who are swift, strong, wise, intelligent, and skilled, he is obviously referring to investment professionals.)

Whatever its other strengths, the human mind seems ill-suited to appreciate the role of chance. So firmly wedded are we to simple everyday notions of cause and effect that even renowned statisticians admit to frequently coming up with answers that later, after more careful analysis, prove incorrect. For the rest of us, the pitfalls in understanding probabilities are even more perilous. I recall overhearing a conversation that began, "The weatherman says there's a ten percent change of rain today." "Well," was the reply, "around here that's about all that it takes."

To see the problem posed by random effects, let's think about how to determine whether a major league batter is more skillful than the average major leaguer. Two problems immediately come to mind. First, how much data do we need to be confident of our answer? It would certainly be unfair to compare his season batting average to the major league average after only a few games. How many appearances at the plate are needed? Second, it's almost always possible to appeal to special circumstances that override whatever conclusion is suggested by the numbers themselves -- injuries, a slow start, lucky catches, especially tough pitchers, and so on. These same difficulties attend comparisons between investment performance and an index.

Even in the absence of special circumstances thought to have affected the result, comparisons between measured performance and an index of some sort are often less informative than one might suppose. Tversky and Kahnemann (1982) have documented a nearly universal human tendency towards overconfidence in such comparisons -- a phenomenon they describe as "belief in the law of small numbers." In fixed-income investing, for example, a portfolio that outperformed by 100 basis points an index it closely resembled would typically be regarded as exhibiting indubitable evidence of its manager's skill. Yet, as Mark Kritzman (1987) has shown, such performance would in fact have to be sustained for *eleven years* before we could be 90% certain that the it reflected skill rather than chance!

In short, measurement error and random effects create almost insuperable obstacles to determining whether a portfolio manager has exhibited superior skill. If *Ecclesiastes* is correct about the role of chance in human affairs, then the later Biblical claim that "by their fruits shall ye know them" has limited validity, at least in fixed-income investment management. Figures may not lie, but they are often silent.

However, as Gertrude Stein might suggest, perhaps this is the wrong question. While an insurer or baseball owner may find it useful to determine whether his team was skillful or just lucky, what really counts is whether they had a winning season. From the standpoint of the firm as a whole, the most important question is whether its value has increased as a consequence of investment results -- regardless of whether those results are the product of chance or skill. Can we, by comparing investment performance to an index, even one that is customized to resemble the firm's liabilities, answer this more significant question?

Unfortunately, we cannot. The principal reason is not random effects, which are irrelevant to this question, or measurement error, which is still present, but the far more serious problem of *omitted variables*. The value of the firm is critically affected by a variable not reflected in any performance measure commonly used: the magnitude of risk to which the portfolio -- and therefore the firm -- is exposed.

The value of any firm is the present (i.e., discounted) value of its future cash inflows and outflows, adjusted for the degree of uncertainty (i.e., risk) in those flows.[6] Risky inflows have a lower present value, and risky outflows a higher present value, than cash flows that are certain. Increasing the magnitude of net future cash flows increases firm value, while increasing their uncertainty reduces it. To determine whether the value of the firm has changed, we therefore need to ascertain what changes have occurred both in the expected magnitude of its future cash flows and in their uncertainty. Unfortunately, *none of the performance measures in common use reflects changes in uncertainty, or risk.*

To be sure, total return does reflect risk that has in fact been realized during the measurement period, through changes in prices. For example, the purchaser of a corporate bond accepts promised cash flows that are higher but more uncertain than those of Treasuries. If the issuer's financial strength significantly declines during the measurement period, the expected cash flows from the bond will be lower, its price will decline, and total return from the bond will consequently be lower than for Treasuries. In this case the risk originally accepted has been partially realized. But if the issuer's financial strength remains unchanged during the period, so will the price of the bond, and the yield premium will likely make total return from the bond exceed that of Treasuries. (As Merton (1974) has demonstrated, purchasing a zero-coupon bond with default risk is equivalent to simultaneously purchasing a Treasury zero with an identical maturity and selling a put on the assets of the issuing firm, with an exercise price equal to the promised payment at maturity. The yield premium over a Treasury reflects the proceeds from selling the put.)

An analogy may help to clarify this point. Suppose that you pay a dollar to play the following game. I will flip a coin ten times. Each

---

[6] The oft-heard pronouncement that only *systematic* (i.e., market-related) risk affects the value of the firm, since individual investors can, by appropriate diversification or hedging, virtually eliminate the effect on their portfolios of risks unique to a particular firm, is true only under extremely restrictive conditions that are seldom met. My own statement applies to a world in which markets are incomplete (i.e., no markets exist for some types of assets -- try selling your pension benefits), securities are traded in lumpy amounts (you can't buy half a share), transactions are costly, and information is both incomplete and costly. For convincing evidence that nonsystematic or diversifiable risk does indeed matter to investors, see Staking (1989) and Babbel and Staking (1989).

time that it comes up heads I owe you a dollar, to be paid at the end of the game. If it comes up tails the game ends and I owe you nothing. This is similar to buying a very risky zero-coupon bond. So long as the coin keeps coming up heads, your total return, book yield, and book income in each period will be impressively high, even though your expected payoff is in fact less than a penny (you have one chance in 1024 to win $10.00). The assumed risk of losing is always present, but is realized only in the period when the coin comes up tails. Only then will these performance measures be adversely affected.

In short, the problem with the performance measures in common use is that they reflect only the risk that has been *realized* during the measurement period, not the risk that has been *assumed*. They tell us how many pigeons have already come home to roost, but not how many more may still be on the way.

If we are concerned about the value of the firm, then, a fundamental problem with performance measures is that they tell us only part of the story. Worse yet, what they tell us can be misleading. In the coin-flipping game just described, so long as one is winning, performance will appear to be stellar -- far greater than for a more prudent investment. In a similar way, the value of investment performance measures can be boosted by increasing investment risk, even though the net effect may be to lower the value of the firm. *This is the paradox of performance measurement: "good" performance may in fact make the firm worse off.*

This paradox is by no means new. It has long been evident that in comparing the performance of equity managers some adjustment for differences in risk exposure is essential, and several have been suggested (Levy and Sarnat. 1984, Ch. 15). Unfortunately, satisfactory risk-adjusted performance measures have not been fully developed for fixed-income portfolios.

In practice, constraints are typically imposed to prevent investment decisions that could boost performance measures by increasing risk exposure. For example, a portfolio manager may be required to maintain the duration and credit quality of the actual portfolio close to those of some index or benchmark portfolio. But to reward a portfolio manager for beating an index while simultaneously constraining the opportunity to do so creates a kind of motivational inconsistency, for it simply channels risk-taking into forms that are less easily observed or measured. As every portfolio manager knows, the way to beat an index under such constraints is to purchase, from the set of securities included in the index, those bonds that are least liquid, that have the greatest call or prepayment risk, and whose credit quality classification is least accurate, so that their yields are atypically high (Fridson, 1990). In short, the resulting portfolio will almost certainly be more risky than the index to which it is compared, but in ways that are difficult to measure. The common practice of rewarding performance while simultaneously limiting how far a portfolio can deviate in its characteristics from an index portfolio thus merely sets a lower bound on risk exposure relative to the index -- not an upper bound, as was intended.

A more extreme solution is to prohibit such deviations entirely, by requiring the portfolio manager to simply replicate an appropriately chosen index portfolio. The challenge to the portfolio manager in this case is not to beat the index but to match it. While this does avoid the motivational problem just described, it ultimately fails to solve the more fundamental problem of controlling risk, which now appears in a different form: how to select an appropriate index. Only an index consisting of Treasury securities whose cash flows are matched to liability payments is truly riskless. In today's competitive environment, such a portfolio would typically be unprofitable (as well as infeasible, if liability cash flows are interest-sensitive). So the problem becomes one of choosing a portfolio or index that has an acceptable combination of risk and expected return. How this can be done is outlined in the next section.

Avoiding the Pitfalls

The late Bertrand Russell was a British philosopher and logician whose book on the logical foundations of mathematics, *Principia Mathematica* (written jointly with Alfred North Whitehead), was an acknowledged masterpiece but so technically difficult that it was fully understood by only a few. Later in life he enjoyed a wide popular following as a brilliant and persuasive essayist. "I'm taken seriously," he once explained, "because everyone knows that I could restate what I've said in a language so difficult and obscure that only two or three other people in the world could understand it. Consequently, if they are tempted to disagree with me, they instead assume I'm saying something terribly profound that they've simply been unable to fully grasp." In a similar vein, let me assure you that much of what I am about to say has its ultimate foundation in a branch of engineering known as stochastic optimal control,[7] which aims at ensuring optimal performance under risk -- that is, under conditions only partly susceptible to human control. However, since space is conveniently limited, I propose that we omit my demonstrating this point with an awesome display of mathematical virtuosity, and skip directly to the part where I speak in plain English and you believe everything I say.

It is common practice in many firms to use performance measurement as a guide to investment decision-making, whether or not it is linked to compensation. Performance that is poor relative to some index or comparison signals the need to alter the decisions being made. In this respect, performance measurement is part of an organizational feedback loop, very much like the thermostat in one's living room. When the measured temperature in the room falls below a target value, a signal is generated that turns on the heat.

As we have just seen, this feedback loop is defective in one crucial respect. The performance measures on which it relies fail to reflect one of the two critical variables that determine the value of the firm. It is possible for decisions that appear to be good ones to in fact be harmful, and for performance measures to tell us that all is well when the value of the firm may in fact be declining. I am by no means asserting that such occurrences are common, but only that the potential exists for this to occur.

The problem is that two critical variables affect the value of the firm, but performance measurement as currently practiced assists us in controlling only one of them. Unfortunately, *this defect is inherent in any performance measure that focuses solely on the past,* because *risk exposure necessarily pertains to the future.* If our aim is to maximize the value of the firm by controlling the riskiness of future cash flows as well

---

[7] For the business reader the best nontechnical introduction is Ackoff (1970), especially Chapter 6: Control. Holt, Modigliani, Muth, and Simon (1960) is an early pathbreaking application to a practical business problem. Technical works include Weyrick (1975), which provides a lucid introduction to the basic concepts of control theory in a deterministic environment, Chow (1975), which gives an accessible treatment of stochastic optimal control in an economic setting, and Stengel (1986), which is a comprehensive but difficult survey. Some applications to finance are collected in Ziemba and Vickson (1975).

as their magnitudes, then *we must broaden our concept and measurement of performance to encompass the future as well as the past.* If the value of the firm reflects both its future as well as its past, then so must our measures of investment performance, if they are to assist us in maximizing firm value. In engineering this is known as *feedforward control*, which might be loosely defined as estimating the future so as to better control it. (As you recall, we agreed to skip a rigorous demonstration.) While measures that incorporate the future must necessarily be imprecise, imprecise measures of the correct variables are more useful than precise measures of the wrong ones.

This last point is exemplified by the incident in which a policeman walking his beat encountered a drunkard crawling under a lamppost, obviously searching for something. "What are you looking for?" inquired the policeman. "My keys," replied the drunkard. "I dropped them." "Just where did you drop them?" inquired the policeman, hoping to be helpful. "Over there in that dark alley," was the response. "But then why are you searching here under the lamppost?" asked the puzzled policeman. Answered the drunkard: "Because there's more light over here." The moral of this story is straightforward: peering into the future may be difficult, but one of the keys to the value of the firm can be found only by doing so.

To put some meat on the rather abstract bones I've offered just now, let me briefly sketch a process of investment decision-making that seeks to control both risk and return, and incorporates both feedback and what I have referred to as feedforward control. Table 2 shows the steps in this process, the critical question that is asked and answered at each step, and some sources of failure that should be avoided.

A. The first step is to select an appropriate *control variable* or objective. Throughout this discussion I have assumed that our aim is to maximize the value of the firm, considered as an ongoing enterprise. It's quite possible, however, for some other objective or combination of objectives to be adopted. The crucial requirement is that the objectives be what we are fundamentally trying to accomplish, and that they be consistent. While it may be tempting to substitute an intermediate objective (earnings growth) for a more fundamental one (growth in the value of the firm), we are all familiar with instances in which intermediate and fundamental objectives conflict

TABLE 2
A Process for Investment Decision-Making

Investment Process	Critical Questions	Sources of Failure
A. Select the *control variable*: the appropriate objective to be achieved	*What* are we trying to accomplish: profit? growth? some combination?	Inappropriate, incompatible, or nonfundamental objectives.
B. Set initial *target value* for this variable	*How much* do we want to accomplish?	Target is infeasible (see E).
C. Specify initial *tolerance for risk*	How much *variation from target value* is acceptable in current and future periods?	Criteria are infeasible (see E) or absent, or pertain to actions rather than objective.
D. *Design alternative investment strategies,* including planned responses to changes in expected conditions.	What investment decisions will achieve the target under expected conditions? What will we do if conditions (e.g., sales or interest rates) deviate from our expectations?	Strategy and planned responses are infeasible or are based on erroneous assumptions concerning markets, clients, liabilities, etc.

Table 2 continued

E. *Test* strategies to estimate future outcome distribution for each. *Adjust* target (B) or tolerance (C) as needed to *select* optimal strategy.	How will each strategy perform under alternative scenarios? Which strategy has the best combination of return and risk (variability)?	Use of limited or unrealistic scenarios to test strategies. Failure to consider whether strategy is vulnerable to changes not explicitly included in scenarios.
F. *Monitor* changes in critical conditions	Have conditions deviated from our assumptions?	Failure to detect or accurately measure critical changes.
G. *Implement* appropriate planned response	What action did we plan in response to this change?	Failure to implement response.
H. *Measure* change in the control variable achieved in preceding period and change in its projected future distribution	Were actual results within the tolerance range we specified? Has the distribution of future results widened or narrowed?	Actual results obscured by error or use of inappropriate measures. Failure to estimate changes in the distribution of future outcomes.
I. *Evaluate* the strategy employed and the process used to implement it	Are changes needed in the strategy adopted or in the process by which it is implemented?	Faulty interpretation of performance measures, faulty diagnosis, or ineffective revisions.

with one another. The increased complexity of and tight coupling between insurer assets and liabilities has made such potential conflicts more prevalent.

B. The second step is to set an initial *target value* for this variable or objective: e.g., 15% growth in the value of the firm over future periods.

C. Third, we specify an initial *tolerance for risk*, for potential deviations from this target value over future periods. Actual results over time will naturally tend to follow a path that wanders about. How far are we willing to let it stray from the target value we have adopted?

D. Fourth, we *design alternative investment strategies*, which should include a specification of our planned responses to changes in expected conditions. Immunization, for example, is a strategy that incorporates periodic rebalancing of the portfolio to maintain a close relationship between assets and liabilities. The design of an immunization strategy would include a specification of how frequently, or under what conditions, such rebalancing would occur, and how it would be accomplished.

E. Fifth, we now *test* these alternative strategies by simulating possible futures. The simulations would permit changes in each of the principal conditions that affect investment decisions and insurance cash flows, and would incorporate appropriate random processes for variables such as interest rates. The simulation should be sufficiently realistic to reflect how portfolio managers, product managers, and customers would behave in response to each simulated path or sequence of changing conditions, and would incorporate plausible interdependencies among their decisions. These repeated simulations permit us to estimate both an *expected outcome* and a *distribution* of future outcomes for each alternative strategy. We now *adjust* our target and our tolerance for deviation so as to *select* the particular strategy whose expected outcome and associated distribution of future outcomes will, we think, most satisfactorily accomplish our objective. This step is crucial, for it permits us to control risk by selecting that strategy with an acceptable distribution of future outcomes as well as an acceptable expected outcome. In short, this step permits us to deliberately and simultaneously choose both the expected magnitude *and variability* of future net cash flows.

F. Having chosen our strategy, we now implement it. To do so requires that we *monitor* changes in critical conditions to which a response is necessary.

G. Next, we *implement* responses to these changes in the manner specified in the strategy we have chosen.

H. At the end of each period, we *measure* what change has occurred in the control variable. Equally important, we now repeat our simulations -- this time only for the strategy we have already adopted -- to determine once again a distribution of future outcomes. Measuring performance now involves asking two questions: (a) was the outcome actually achieved within the tolerance range we specified? and **(b) has the distribution of future outcomes remained acceptable? If this distribution has widened, the firm's risk exposure has increased. If it has narrowed, risk has been reduced.** This step is crucial, because it measures the firm's risk exposure and informs us of changes in it.

I. Finally, we *evaluate* both the strategy we have selected and the process by which we have implemented it, to determine whether changes are needed and how they might be brought about.

If, as I have assumed, our aim is to maximize the value of our firms, then a process similar to the one just described is essential, for only in this way can we estimate and control the risk to which our firms are exposed.

Is this really feasible? I assure you it is, for comparable simulations of complex, interdependent cash flows that are only partially predictable are performed daily both on Wall Street and in the investment departments of some insurers to price and manage mortgage-backed securities and products derived from them. Were Van Winkle, our well-rested portfolio manager from 1970, to visit these firms, he would be astonished by the new concepts and analytical techniques that have been developed and the products they have engendered. Let me simply mention just a few of them:

> PIKs and PIPs, TACs and PACs,
> Fannie Maes and Freddie Macs,
> OAS, binomial tree,
> Term structure of volatility,
>
> IOs, POs, gnomes and TANs,
> TIGRs, CATs, dwarfs and RANs,
> PSA, arbitrage-free,
> Theta, put-call parity,
>
> D1, D2, D3, D4,
> Swaption, Collar, Cap and Floor,
> Cubic splines, lognormality,
> Dynamic hedging, risk neutrality,
>
> Ito's lemma, Altman's Z,
> Delta, gamma, APT,
> Mean reversion, path-dependency,
> Autoregressive conditional heteroskedasticity.

My recommendation thus requires that we take a technology *already in use* for managing assets and adapt it intelligently to the management of the firm as a whole -- its liabilities as well as its assets.

But aren't our products too complex and our customers too unpredictable for this to be feasible? Whenever this question is asked I am reminded of the country banker in Vermont who was sitting at his desk one day when a farmer came in and asked to borrow a dollar. The banker was surprised at the small amount, but agreed, provided that the farmer would supply collateral for the deal. "Will this be enough?" asked the farmer, pulling from his pocket a sheaf of government bonds. "That's fine," said the banker, "but you'll have to pay 10% interest." The farmer agreed, handed the banker the bonds and a dime, took the dollar, and went his way. A year later he returned and renewed the loan, paying another ten cents. A year after that, when he again asked to renew the loan, the banker could no longer contain his curiosity. "It's very peculiar that you, with all those bonds, still keep renewing a one dollar loan," he observed. "Well," said the farmer, "it's peculiar that you haven't figured it out. I was paying ten dollars a year for a safe deposit box for my bonds. Now I've found a way to keep them safe for only ten cents."

I certainly agree that our products and customers exhibit complexities far greater than this. But that merely increases our need to systematically measure and control our risk exposure. If we fail to do so, we may find that we, like this banker, have failed to adequately price and manage our products. In short, while we should by no means underestimate the potential difficulties in what I propose, neither should we let them blind us to our need to better control risk, or to the increased opportunities to do so created by new concepts and tools.

Summary

1. During the past two decades, the insurance industry has become more competitive, thus eroding profit margins, while insurance products and the securities purchased to fund them have become both more complex and more tightly linked to one another. Finally, securities markets have become more volatile. Because of these changes, our industry is exposed to greater risk.

2. Unfortunately, the measures commonly used by insurers to evaluate fixed-income investment performance are insensitive to changes in risk exposure. Consequently, although overall risk exposure has increased, the problem of measuring and managing risk exposure has been given little attention until recently.

3. The value of an insurer is the present value of its expected future cash flows, adjusted for risk. Other things equal, an increase in its risk exposure reduces firm value.

4. The paradox of performance measurement is that there is no necessary or close relationship between the performance measures in common use and changes in the value of the firm. Investment decisions that reduce firm value (by increasing risk exposure) can appear to be

"good" ones by these measures, while decisions that increase firm value (by reducing risk) may not, if they fail to affect current income.

5.   Because risk exposure necessarily pertains to the future, this defect is inherent in any performance measure that focuses solely on the past. It can be remedied only by constructing measures that reflect the potential variability of future cash flows. While such measures will necessarily be imprecise, an imprecise measure of the correct variable is more useful than a precise measure of the wrong one.

6.   Fortunately, the increased complexity and volatility of securities markets has been accompanied by a simultaneous increase in conceptual and technical sophistication. The concepts and tools now used to price and manage complex securities can, in principle, be adapted to managing the price and risk of both assets and liabilities, so as to maximize the value of the firm as a whole.

Conclusion: Financial Management as Engineering

The great benefit of eclecticism is that it enlarges the opportunity for serendipity. In my own case it led to the discovery of previously unsuspected relationships between two professions -- engineering and financial management -- that would appear to be unrelated. In my introduction, you may recall, I suggested that our industry is changing in ways that make it more closely resemble technology-intensive industries, and I later hinted that some of my remarks could be restated in form known to engineers as stochastic optimal control. Although sufficient detail to make these suggestions more convincing is not appropriate here, I am by no means unique in perceiving them, for another contributor to this symposium, Clifford Smith, has co-edited a book entitled *The Handbook of Financial Engineering.*

There is, however, another resemblance that is more important, more substantive, and more easily described.   Although the raw materials from which they are built are clearly different, life insurance products, like buildings, bridges, planes, and power plants, are *supposed to last* -- sometimes for fifty, sixty, or even seventy years. Portfolio managers, like engineers, share in the responsibility of making good on that promise. I take this to be one of the many implications of the statement by Charles Ellis (1985), in his now-classic book *Investment Policy,* that "portfolio management is investment engineering (p. 50)." For engineers, as Henry Petroski (1985) points out in *To Engineer is Human,* creating things that will last requires that "engineering design has as its first and foremost objective the obviation of failure" (p. xii).   "[I]t is as much the designer's business to know how any structure might fail as it is a chess player's to know how one false move may lead to checkmate" (p. 186).   The essence of successful engineering design, then, lies in *"foreseeing failure"* -- in "predicting the forces to which a structure may be subjected at any time in the future" -- a task that "must often deal in probabilities and combinations of probabilities" (p. 41).   Because it supports products that are supposed to last, portfolio management must likewise be, as Ellis describes it, "a *defensive* process."   "The basic responsibility of portfolio managers . . . is to control and manage risk (p. 52)."

If we, like engineers, are to offer products that last, then we must likewise carry out the difficult but essential task of predicting the forces to which our firms -- our products and the assets that support them -- may be subjected in the future.   The changes in our industry and our environment make this task more difficult than ever before, but also more crucial.   Designing, testing, and evaluating investment strategies with respect to alternative future events therefore lies at the very heart of the investment management process I have outlined.   And because this task similarly focuses on the future rather than the past, we, like engineers, "must often deal in probabilities and combinations of probabilities."   Implementing such a process will by no means be simple, and will require many of us to learn new ways of thinking about our business.   But doing so is more than just "a nice idea in principle."   It is what we *must* do to keep our promises.

REFERENCES

Ackoff, Russell, 1970, *A Concept of Corporate Planning* (New York: John Wiley and Sons).

Babbel, David F., and Kim B. Staking, 1989, The Market Reward for Insurers That Practice Asset/Liability Management, New York, Goldman Sachs.

Babbel, David F., Robert Stricker, and Irwin T. Vanderhoof, 1990, Performance Measurement for Insurers, New York, Goldman Sachs.

Chow, Gregory C., 1975, *Analysis and Control of Dynamic Economic Systems* (New York: John Wiley and Sons).

Dietz, Peter O., and Jeannette R. Kirschman, 1983, Evaluating Portfolio Performance, in John L. Maginn and Donald L. Tuttle, eds., *Managing Investment Portfolios: A Dynamic Process* (Boston: Warren, Gorham, and Lamont).

Ellis, Charles D., 1985, *Investment Policy* (Homewood, IL: Dow Jones-Irwin).

Fridson, Martin S., 1990, Performance Measurement in High Yield Bonds, New York, Morgan Stanley.

Holt, Charles C., Franco Modligliani, John F. Muth, and Herbert A. Simon, 1960, Planning Production, Inventories, and Work Force (Englewood Cliffs, N.J.: Prentice-Hall).

Kritzman, Mark P., 1987, Incentive Fees: Some Problems and Some Solutions, *Financial Analysts Journal*, January-February, 21-26.

Levy, Haim, and Marshall Sarnat, 1984, *Portfolio and Investment Selection: Theory and Practice* (Englewood Cliffs, NJ: Prentice-Hall International).

Lynch, John J., Jr., and Jan H. Mayle, 1986, *Standard Securities Calculation Methods: Fixed Income Securities Formulas* (New York: Securities Industry Association).

Merrill Lynch, 1985, A Guide to the Merrill Lynch Taxable Bond Indices, New York, Merrill Lynch.

Merton, Robert C., 1974, On the Pricing of Corporate Debt: The Risk Structure of Interest Rates, *Journal of Finance*, 29: 449-70. Reprinted in Merton, 1990, *Continuous-Time Finance* (Cambridge: Blackwell), 388-412.

Perrow, Charles, 1984, *Normal Accidents: Living with High-Risk Technologies* (New York: Basic Books).

Petroski, Henry, 1985, *To Engineer is Human: The Role of Failure in Successful Design* (New York: St. Martin's Press).

Reese, Stuart and Laurent Guy, 1990, Fixed Income Portfolio Performance: Myth Versus Reality (unpublished manuscript).

Smith, Clifford W., Jr., and Charles W. Smithson, eds., 1990, *The Handbook of Financial Engineering* (New York: Harper Business).

Staking, Kim, 1989, Interest Rate Sensitivity and the Value of Surplus: Duration Mismatch in the Property-Liability Insurance Industry, Unpublished dissertation, University of Pennsylvania, Philadelphia, PA.

Stengel, Robert F., 1986, *Stochastic Optimal Control: Theory and Application* (New York: John Wiley and Sons).

Tversky, Amos, and Daniel Kahneman, 1982, Belief in the Law of Small Numbers, in Daniel Kahneman, Paul Slovic, and Amos Tversky, eds., *Judgment under Uncertainty: Heuristic and Biases* (Cambridge: Cambridge University Press).

Weyrick, Robert C., 1975, *Fundamentals of Automatic Control* (New York: McGraw-Hill).

Williams, Arthur III, 1983, Performance Evaluation in Fixed Income Securities, in Frank J. Fabozzi and Irving M. Pollack, eds., *The Handbook of Fixed Income Securities* (Homewood, IL: Dow Jones-Irwin).

Williams, Arthur III and Noreen M. Conwell, 1983, Fixed Income Indices, in Frank J. Fabozzi and Irving M. Pollack, eds., *The Handbook of Fixed Income Securities* (Homewood, IL: Dow Jones-Irwin).

Ziemba, W. T., and R. G. Vickson, 1975, *Stochastic Optimization Models in Finance* (New York: Academic Press).

6 ESTIMATING DIVISIONAL COST OF CAPITAL FOR INSURANCE COMPANIES

Franklin Allen

Professor of Finance and Economics
Vice Dean and Director
Wharton Doctoral Programs
The Wharton School
University of Pennsylvania

1. Introduction

In a competitive market, what should the rate of return on insurance companies' equity be? What premiums should insurance companies charge? Traditionally, the answers to these questions have been based on actuarial and accounting concepts.[1] More recently financial models of the insurance firm have been developed. Ferrari (1968) suggested a descriptive model which allowed an algebraic expression for the rate of return on equity as a function of the premiums charged to be derived. Combining this with the capital asset pricing model (CAPM) meant that an equilibrium value for the return on equity

---

I am grateful to David Cummins for helpful discussions and comments. Financial support from the NSF is acknowledged.

[1] See, for example, Cummins and Chang (1983).

and the corresponding level of premiums could be found. This model is known as the insurance CAPM.[2] The development of other asset pricing models in finance has also led to insurance counterparts. Thus the Arbitrage Pricing Theory, and option pricing models have been used to derive the return on equity and the level of premiums.[3] Although the approaches based on asset pricing models have advantages compared to those based on traditional actuarial and accounting concepts, they are not ideal. One of the most important problems is that they are not well suited for finding premiums when an insurance company has multiple divisions. The difficulty is that it is not clear how earnings on reserves should be allocated among the various divisions of the firm.

The other financial method of pricing insurance is the Discounted Cash Flow approach. There are two versions of this. Myers and Cohn (1987) have suggested an adaptation of the adjusted present value method for calculating the price of insurance. The premium is found by discounting the expected cash flows associated with the insurance at the appropriate discount rates. The other method is the NCCI (1987) approach which uses an internal rate of return methodology. This involves finding the discount rate such that the net discounted cash flow is zero. The fair premium is the one such that this discount rate is equal to the opportunity cost of capital. Cummins (1990c) shows that these models are essentially the same if properly applied and the choice between them is a question of which is easier to use. Unfortunately, as with the approaches based on asset pricing models, neither of these methods is well suited to finding insurance premiums when a company has multiple divisions. The problem is again how to deal with reserves and allocate the earnings from these to the different divisions.

Existing financial methods of pricing insurance take the structure of the insurance firm as given. It is argued below that a more fruitful approach is to start with the question of why insurance firms have the particular structure that they do. In an ideal world there would be no need for insurance companies to be involved in financial markets. If contracts were costlessly enforceable, it would not be necessary for

---

[2] See Cooper (1974), Biger and Kahane (1978), Fairley (1979) and Hill (1979).

[3] For surveys of this literature see D'Arcy and Doherty (1988) and Cummins (1990a; 1990b).

premiums to be paid in advance. Instead, premiums could be paid by those that did not suffer losses at the time when payouts were necessary. In this case, the insurance company would simply be a conduit for premiums from those who did not suffer any loss to those who did.

In practice, of course, this type of insurance company could not survive because contracts are not costlessly enforceable. It would be very difficult, if not impossible, to force the people who did not suffer a loss to make payments. For this reason, insurance companies require payment for insurance at the beginning of the period rather than at the end. It is this problem which causes insurance companies to be involved in financial markets since they invest the premiums they receive until payouts are necessary.

Although the case where payments are made at the end of the period is unrealistic, it is nevertheless important as a benchmark. It means the insurance aspects of the problem can be separated from the investment aspects. Among other things, this allows the level of premiums to be determined when an insurance company has multiple divisions. It also allows a theory of the competitive rate of return on insurance companies' equity to be developed.

Section 2 starts with the benchmark case where there are perfect contracts and capital markets. Section 3 considers what happens if contracting possibilities are imperfect but capital markets are perfect. In Section 4, imperfect capital markets are introduced into the analysis. Section 5 focuses on the role of shareholders, Section 6 introduces risky insurance liabilities and Section 7 considers the effect of taxes. Finally, Section 8 contains conclusions.

2. Perfect Contracts and Capital Markets

If contracts are costlessly enforceable, insurance firms will not need to collect premiums until losses are incurred. This benchmark case is analyzed first. Frictionless capital markets and advance collection of premiums are then introduced.

Perfect Contracts

Initially, consider a simple scenario. There are two dates $t = 0$, 1. The number of consumers is very large. They all have the same initial wealth and the same opportunities. They are risk averse with identical utility functions $U(W_1)$ where $U' > 0$, $U'' < 0$ and W_1 is wealth at date 1.

At date 0, each faces a probability π ($0<\pi<1$) of a loss L at date 1 so the expected loss is EL = πL. This loss is observable to an insurance company. The risks consumers face are independent so that the standard error of their average loss is zero. Every consumer is made better off by insuring against the risk and guaranteeing a level of consumption of W_1 - EL.

The loss can be thought of as a property loss such as a house burning down. An alternative interpretation is that households are the relevant unit and one of the members of the household dies with a resultant loss in earning power. The model is thus applicable to both property and to life insurance.

As far as the insurance industry is concerned, there are no barriers to entry, the market is competitive and there are no costs in setting up and running an insurance company. This implies that profits will be zero in equilibrium. The prices referred to below are equilibrium prices.

There is *perfect* contracting in the sense that all contracts are costlessly enforceable. As a result, insurance companies can ensure that everybody receives W_1 - EL at date 1 by issuing contracts of the following form. At date 0, before consumers know whether they will suffer a loss or not, they sign a contract promising to pay EL at date 1 if they do not suffer a loss. In return, the insurance company will promise to pay L-EL to all those consumers who do suffer a loss at date 1. In this way the risk associated with the loss L can be entirely eliminated and consumers' welfare is maximized. Competition among the insurance companies ensures that payments are set at this level and their profits are zero since revenues are $(1-\pi)$EL and costs are π(L-EL) = $(1-\pi)$EL.

This equilibrium will be referred to as the *benchmark* equilibrium. Its assumptions essentially correspond to the Arrow-Debreu framework and the allocation that results is therefore Pareto efficient.

In the simple case presented, the only issue in pricing the insurance is the expected loss. There is no need for a cost of capital because all payments are made at the same time.

The insurance contracts with payments at date 1 do not, of course, correspond to actual insurance contracts where payments are required before the insurance starts. The reason that advance payments are necessary in practice, is obviously that contracts are not costlessly enforceable. It would be very difficult for insurance companies to make those consumers who do not suffer a loss pay EL at date 1. This problem is overcome by requiring all consumers to pay a premium at date 0 and then making payouts to those consumers suffering a loss at date 1. The complication that this introduces is that the premiums can be invested in financial markets between dates 0 and 1. Section 3 examines the effect of relaxing the assumption that contracts are perfectly enforceable. However, before doing this it is helpful to consider what happens if capital markets are introduced into the analysis and premiums are paid at date 0.

Perfect Capital Markets

Suppose that in addition to perfect contracting, capital markets are *perfect*. In other words, all agents have equal access so both firms and consumers face the same interest rates and investment opportunities. There is no difference between borrowing and lending rates, all agents have the same information, the market is perfectly competitive, there are no transaction costs and so forth. In addition, markets are complete so that there are full risk sharing possibilities. There are no taxes.

In these circumstances, there are a number of different types of insurance contract which allow consumers to eliminate the risk associated with the loss L. One alternative is the benchmark case where insurance contracts are signed at date 0 but all payments are made at date 1. In addition to arranging insurance at date 0, consumers use their initial wealth to purchase an optimal portfolio Z^*. The ex post return on this portfolio is denoted R^* and the expected return is ER^*. At date 1, consumers use the proceeds from their investment to pay out EL if they did not suffer a loss. If they did suffer a loss they receive L-EL from the insurance company. Their total wealth at date 1 is therefore R^*-EL whatever happens. Consumers thus have insurance against the loss L they face and so do not have to bear any of this risk but they do bear an optimal amount of investment risk.[4]

The existence of perfect capital markets means that an alternative arrangement is for premiums to be paid at date 0 and for the insurance companies to invest them. The interest and dividends earned ensures a premium lower than EL will be charged. For example, suppose the premiums were invested in a risk free asset yielding r_F. In this case the premium at date 0, denoted p_0, could be set at

---

[4] See Chapter 4 of Sharpe (1970) for an analysis of optimal risk bearing by investors.

$$p_0 = \frac{EL}{1 + r_F} \qquad (1)$$

and the company would still have sufficient funds to cover its liabilities. However, notice that the allocation of resources would be exactly the same as before. The only difference would be that policyholders would reduce their holdings of the risk free asset by $EL/(1+r_F)$ between dates 0 and 1 and would pay the premium a period earlier.

This is just an application of the well-known Modigliani and Miller (1958) result from corporate finance. The theorem asserts that with perfect and complete capital markets the value of a firm does not depend on its capital structure because investors' opportunity sets are not affected by its capital structure. If the firm takes on more debt, for example, shareholders will not be any better off because if they had wanted levered equity they could have borrowed on their own account.

In the insurance context, policyholders can offset any action of the insurance company in terms of the timing of the premium by adjusting their holding of the risk free asset appropriately. No matter what the spread of payments between dates 0 and 1 the policyholder's opportunity set and hence the allocation of resources will not be affected. What happens if an insurance company were to require a premium at date 0 and instead of investing it in the risk free asset invested it in a risky asset with random rate of return r and mean rate of return Er? The insurance company could charge a premium

$$p_0 = \frac{EL}{1 + Er} \qquad (2)$$

and on average have enough to cover its liabilities. The "on average" is important here since some of the time the realization of r will be such that they have more funds than they require to meet their liabilities and other times there will be a shortfall. In order to ensure they can always meet their liabilities, companies can use contracts which require policyholders to make extra payments when there is a shortfall. Any surplus at date 1 can be paid out to policyholders. To see how this might work, suppose the funds an insurance company has available at date 1 as a result of investing the premiums at date 0 are αEL. If $\alpha < 1$, those who did not suffer a loss would be required to pay $(1-\alpha)EL$ each and those who did suffer a loss would receive $L-(1-\alpha)EL$. If $\alpha > 1$, those who do not suffer a loss receive a refund of (α-1)EL and those who do suffer a loss receive L-(1-α)EL > L-EL.

Are the policyholders any better off because of the reduction in the average premium? The Modigliani-Miller analysis is again applicable here. Since markets are complete, all that would happen is that the policyholders would alter their portfolios to offset the position the insurance company takes. For example, if an insurance company with N policyholders invests a total of X in a security, each policyholder would reduce his or her investment in that security by x = X/N. Overall, the allocation of resources would be the same as in the benchmark equilibrium when all insurance payments are made at date 1. Policyholders would consume the same amount for every possible realization of r and the insurance company would make zero profits. This discussion gives the following result.

The Insurance Modigliani and Miller Theorem

If insurance contracts are perfectly enforceable, capital markets are perfect and complete and there are no taxes, an insurance company's investment strategy does not affect its policyholders' welfare.

One immediate corollary of this result is that even when there is only one type of loss being insured there is more than one level of premium that is optimal. An equivalent way of putting this is that the cost of capital at which firms should discount expected liabilities to arrive at the breakeven premium is not unique. It depends on the investment strategy the firm has decided to pursue but does not affect policyholders welfare since they will simply take offsetting positions. When there are multiple divisions in the insurance company, the same result will be true. There will be no sense in which there is a unique optimal premium or a well-defined divisional cost of capital.

3. Imperfect Contracts and Perfect Capital Markets

In this section the case where payments at date 1 cannot be enforced but capital markets are perfect is considered. In the previous section there were many different policies that an insurance company could follow. One of these policies stands out in the current context. It guarantees that there will be no shortfall of funds at date 1 so the fact that payments can only be collected at date 0 does not affect its feasibility. Suppose the insurance company charges a premium

$$p_0 = \frac{EL}{1 + r_F} \qquad (3)$$

at date 0 and invests all its funds in the risk free asset. At date 1 it pays out L to all those who suffer a loss and nothing to those who do not. In this case there is no risk that it cannot meet its liabilities. Moreover, the allocation of resources is the same as the benchmark case when payments at date 1 are costlessly enforceable. The policyholders simply adjust their holdings of the risk free asset to offset the fact that the insurance company is effectively investing in the risk free asset on their behalf. They bear the same degree of capital market risk as they do in the benchmark equilibrium where all contracts are fully enforceable.

The cost of capital the insurance company should use in this case in determining its premium is the risk free rate. This is true if it has one division or many divisions.

The other important point here is that investing in the risk free asset is the best thing an insurance company can do for its policyholders. Investing in risky assets may allow it to lower its premium but this will not affect the welfare of its policyholders. To see this, consider what would happen if an insurance company were to invest the premiums in risky assets with expected rate of return $Er > r_F$ and with lower bound on the return of $0 < 1+r_l < 1+r_F$. To ensure that it can meet its liabilities at date 1 it must charge a premium of

$$p_0 = \frac{EL}{1 + r_l} > \frac{EL}{1 + r_F}. \qquad (4)$$

Except when the realized rate of return is r_l, the insurance company will be able to refund part of the dividends to its policyholders. The average effective cost of the insurance in date 0 dollars, denoted c_0, will be

$$c_0 = \frac{EL}{1 + Er} < \frac{EL}{1 + r_F}. \qquad (5)$$

The important point here is that even though the average effective premium is lowered, none of the firm's policyholders are made better off. They will simply adjust their portfolios to offset the investments made by the insurance company. Thus with perfect and complete capital markets the insurance company cannot do any better than invest in the risk free asset and use the risk free rate as its divisional cost of capital.

4. Imperfect Contracts and Capital Markets

The next obvious case to consider is what happens when there are imperfect capital markets and all policyholders cannot simply adjust their portfolios to offset the investment strategy of insurance companies. The imperfections that are likely to lead to this are when policyholders can only borrow at rates in excess of r_F and short sales entail transaction costs; in extreme cases they will not be able to borrow or short sell at all.

For those policyholders who hold sufficient quantities of the risk free asset in their portfolios, the analysis in the previous section remains valid. They will reduce their investment in the risk free asset to offset the effect of paying a premium at date 0. In equilibrium, insurance companies will offer this clientele of consumers a policy with a premium and effective cost of

$$p_0 = c_0 = \frac{EL}{1 + r_F} \qquad (6)$$

and will invest the proceeds in the risk free asset.

What about consumers who do not hold sufficient quantities of the risk free asset to do this? They will not be able to adjust their portfolios to perfectly offset the insurance companies' actions if the only policy that is offered corresponds to investing premiums in the risk free asset. It will be necessary to offer these people a different policy. Suppose these consumers all hold an optimal portfolio Z^*, with expected rate of return ER^* and a lower bound on the return of $1+R_l > 0$. In order to guarantee it can meet its liabilities the insurance company must charge a premium of

$$p_0 = \frac{EL}{1 + R_l}. \qquad (7)$$

As in the example in the previous section, it will also refund any return on the investment portfolio above $1+R_l$ to consumers. Hence the expected cost of insurance in date 0 dollars is

$$c_0 = \frac{EL}{1 + ER^*}. \tag{8}$$

In this case, consumers are made strictly better off by insurance companies offering this policy in addition to the risk free policy. They can now adjust their portfolio to offset the investments of their insurance company and can have the overall portfolio that is optimal for them. Consumers would make this adjustment by reducing their holdings of the optimal portfolio by p_0 since this is the amount the insurance company is effectively investing on their behalf.

What happens if consumers have different optimal portfolios because, for example, their degree of risk aversion or level of wealth differs? In equilibrium, competition ensures each group of consumers will be offered a policy tailored for its particular preferences. Premiums will be set to guarantee that the company can meet its liabilities and the investment policy of the firm will mirror the optimal portfolio of the clientele the policy is designed for. The expected cost of the insurance will depend on the expected return of the consumers' optimal portfolio.

The analysis thus indicates that when there are multiple groups the same type of insurance will be priced differently both in terms of the premium and the expected cost even though the risk of loss that is being insured is the same. Even when there is one division there will therefore be many values for the discount rate, or cost of capital, to be applied to expected liabilities. Essentially it is policyholders that bear the investment risk and the appropriate discount rate is their opportunity cost of capital.[5] The premium has to be paid at date 0 because of the enforceability problem. However, the insurance company is effectively acting on each policyholder's behalf and is investing the premium in assets the policyholder would have invested in if there were no enforceability problem.

In the scheme described, the premium is set at a sufficiently high level to ensure that there will be no shortfall. In practice, the situation where it is perhaps easiest to do this is life insurance. Here the policies

---

[5] It is the policyholders' opportunity cost of capital that is relevant here rather than the equityholders' since the policyholders are providing the funds to be invested. The case where equityholders provide funds is discussed below.

typically last for many years and the probability of a claim is low initially. This means that even with moderate premiums it is relatively easy to build up a surplus. When the policy eventually expires the surplus can be returned to the policyholder.

5. The Role of Insurance Company Equityholders

In the analysis of Section 4, it is assumed that there is a lower bound $1+R_1 > 0$ on the returns to consumers' optimal portfolios. By setting a premium of $p_0 = EL/(1+R_1)$ it is possible to guarantee that the company can meet its liabilities. If $1+R_1$ is small this premium could be large and might exceed the available wealth of the consumers the insurance is targeted at. If $1+R_1 = 0$ it will clearly be impossible to charge a premium which will guarantee that liabilities can be met. How can a company meet its obligations in these situations?

Insurance companies have been modelled so far as competitive firms which make zero profits no matter what happens. The owners or equityholders of the companies have not played a role at all. When there is a possibility of a shortfall this is no longer the case. The equityholders will have to bear this risk and will receive an appropriate return to compensate them.

How would such equityholder guarantees work in practice? One possibility is for there to be unlimited liability and for the equityholders to guarantee to make good any shortfall that occurs at date 1. In Sections 2 and 3 it was argued that it would not be possible in practice to write contracts with policyholders requiring those that do not suffer a loss to make a payment at date 1. In contrast, with insurance company equityholders this type of contract is observed. In essence this is the way that Lloyd's of London operates. People above a certain threshold of wealth apply to be "names" and pledge all their wealth to make good any shortfall when claims come due. Since the wealth threshold is set at a high level the costs of enforcing payment at date 1 are relatively low.[6] Thus the system where equityholders' payments occur at date 1 is of interest in its own right. As in Section 2 it is also of interest as a benchmark.

---

[6] Recent problems in the Lloyd's insurance market have led to resistance by some names to paying the amount they have been called on for. This suggests the costs of enforcing ex post payments are increasing.

The people that bear the residual liability in a Lloyd's type of system receive income to compensate them. Suppose the residual risk is represented by the random variable ε with mean $E\varepsilon$ and variance σ_ε^2. The income received by the people that bear this risk has two components. The first is to compensate them for the expected residual risk and is just $E\varepsilon$. The second is to compensate them for the remainder of the risk. It is shown in the Appendix, which contains an analysis of the market for residual risk, that for small risks this component will only depend on σ_ε^2. If the price that is paid for each unit of variance borne is Θ, the amount that is given at date 1 to compensate the person for bearing the risk is

$$y_1 = E\varepsilon + \Theta\sigma_\varepsilon^2. \tag{9}$$

It is also shown in the Appendix that the demand for residual risk by individuals is Θ/a where a is the person's coefficient of absolute risk aversion. The equilibrium value of Θ is the value such that the demand for bearing residual risk is equal to supply. If the risk borne is large, the income required to compensate for the residual risk will also depend on the third and higher moments of ε. In the analysis below it is assumed that only mean and variance are of any importance.

In equilibrium, the price Θ ensures that people are willing to bear the risk. It will depend on the extent to which the risk can be diversified away. When everybody is well diversified, as in the CAPM, Θ will be zero if the risk is diversifiable but nonzero if it is correlated with market risk. In practice, it appears that most investors are not very well diversified. Blume, Crockett and Friend (1974) found that the average amount of diversification is equivalent to having an equally weighted portfolio with two stocks. Blume and Friend (1978) provide more detailed evidence of this lack of diversification; they find that a large proportion of investors have only one or two stocks and very few have more than ten. One possible explanation of this lack of diversification is that there is a fixed set up cost of participating in a market.[7] Whatever the reason, if investors are not well diversified Θ will be positive.

The theory presented suggests that mutual insurance companies are feasible when $(1+R_l)$ is sufficiently large that the guaranteeing

---

[7] See Allen and Gale (1991) for a discussion of the evidence for lack of diversification and possible reasons for it.

premium can be afforded by many consumers. However, if $1+R_1 = 0$ or is small so the guaranteeing premium $EL/(1+R_1)$ would be too large to be affordable, equityholders will be necessary for the insurance company. Consider how the required payment for the residual risk borne by equityholders affects the pricing of insurance. Policyholders must compensate the equityholders for bearing the residual liability.

In the current framework the reason residual risk arises is that the insurance company is acting as the policyholder's agent in investing the premium between dates 0 and 1. If a cost must be paid for this residual risk it may be that the policyholder's optimal portfolio is changed so that less risk is borne. In some cases it may be that they prefer a policy where the insurance company bears no risk and always invests the premiums in the risk free asset. For example, if markets are complete there will be no advantage from insurance company equityholders bearing the risk. However, in general, when markets are incomplete both equityholders and policyholders will bear risk.

The other decision concerns the level of the premium. The higher the premium the lower the equityholders' residual risk and hence the less compensation that must be paid by policyholders. The level of the premium will be determined by the ability of the policyholder to tie up wealth in the hands of the insurance company relative to the cost of compensating equityholders for the residual risk they bear. If there are constraints on borrowing and short sales, the ability of policyholders to pay large premiums may be severely limited and this may often be the determinant of the level of premiums.

Suppose the mean of the residual risk borne by the equityholders given the optimal premium and the optimal investment strategy for the policyholders' funds is μ and the variance is σ^2. Then the policyholders must pay $\mu+\Theta\sigma^2$ at date 1. The average cost of the insurance in date 0 dollars will be

$$c_0 = \frac{EL}{1 + ER^*} + \frac{\mu + \Theta\sigma^2}{1 + r_F}. \tag{10}$$

Notice that this assumes that the part of the premium to cover liabilities, $EL/(1+ER^*)$, is being held on the policyholders' behalf and is invested at expected return ER^*. The part of the premium to cover the cost of the residual risk, $(\mu+\Theta\sigma^2)/(1+r_F)$, is held on the equityholders' behalf. For simplicity, it is assumed these equityholders do not face any capital market imperfections and it is therefore optimal (i.e. as good as any other strategy) to invest it in the risk free asset.

As far as the level of the premium is concerned, it will depend on the amount of residual risk that it is optimal for equityholders to bear. In general, the higher the premium the less residual risk equityholders will bear and the smaller $\mu + \Theta\sigma^2$ will be.

The cost of capital (i.e. the value liabilities should be discounted at) corresponding to c_0 in (10) is the value of γ such that

$$\frac{EL}{1 + \gamma} = \frac{EL}{1 + ER^*} + \frac{\mu + \Theta\sigma^2}{1 + r_F}. \tag{11}$$

As before, there is not necessarily a single cost of capital even when there is one type of loss being insured. Policies are designed for particular clienteles and the cost of capital used in pricing the insurance will be clientele specific. When there are multiple divisions this will be true for each division.

Apart from a Lloyd's-type system of equityholder payments at date 1, the other way to guarantee that an insurance company can meet its liabilities is for the shareholders to put up the necessary wealth at date 0 to guarantee payments at date 1. Similarly to Section 2, this avoids the problem of securing payment from them after the event. Conceptually, the surplus is being held on behalf of the equityholders. If it is not required at date 1 to meet insurance liabilities it is returned to them. These funds should therefore be invested on their behalf. As in Section 2, if the equityholders do not face any capital market imperfections or incompleteness a Modigliani-Miller type of analysis is again relevant. The precise way these funds are invested will be irrelevant as far as the shareholders' welfare is concerned because they will be able to take offsetting positions; if the insurance company buys x of a security per shareholder, each shareholder reduces their holding of it by x. Given the purpose of the funds is to assure liabilities at date 1 can be met, investing the surplus in the risk free asset is prudent. If equityholders face capital market imperfections then investing in risky assets on their behalf may simply result in the necessity of putting up more funds at date 0 to guarantee liabilities at date 1. For simplicity, it will be assumed below that all the surplus held on behalf of equityholders is invested in the risk free asset.

The crucial point here is that the funds are held by the insurance company to overcome problems of collection at date 1. In terms of compensating equityholders for bearing the residual risk, the analysis for the Lloyd's type of situation is still valid.   The equityholders in the insurance company will require compensation in the same way and the premium and cost of capital will be calculated as above.   Thus the return on the surplus collected at date 0 to guarantee payment of liabilities at date 1 should not be factored into the premium at all.   The cost that is important for the premium is that incurred in bearing residual risk.

The expected return that shareholders receive is a combination of the expected return earned on surplus held by the insurance company on their behalf and the compensation for bearing the residual risk.   For example, if shareholders put up a guaranteeing surplus of G (and these funds are invested in the risk free asset) the expected fair rate of return r_E would be given by

$$r_E = \frac{(1 + r_f)G + \mu + \Theta\sigma^2}{G} - 1. \qquad (12)$$

An implication of this analysis is that the issue of how to allocate earnings on surplus to particular types of policy or divisions does not arise.   What is important in determining the cost of insurance in different divisions is the residual liability that equityholders bear.   What is important in determining the fair rate of return to equityholders is that they are appropriately compensated for the residual risk they bear.   For example, suppose that a company has two divisions.   The residual risk in division i (= 1, 2) has mean μ_i and variance σ_i^2. If the expected loss being insured in division i is EL_i and the expected return on the portfolio the premiums are invested in is ER_i^*, the average cost of the insurance would be

$$c_{0i} = \frac{EL_i}{1 + ER_i^*} + \frac{\mu + \Theta\sigma_i^2}{1 + r_F}. \qquad (13)$$

The fair rate of return for shareholders who put up a total G of guaranteeing surplus is

$$r_E = \frac{(1 + r_F)G + \mu_1 + \Theta\sigma_1^2 + \mu_2 + \Theta\sigma_2^2}{G} - 1. \tag{14}$$

The extension to the case where there are more than two policies or divisions is straightforward.

6. Risky Insurance Liabilities

An important assumption of the analysis above is that the risks that are insured can be pooled so that overall the risk is eliminated. In many situations this may be an appropriate assumption. However, in others it may not. Even after pooling the policies, there may be residual risk. How does this affect the analysis of the cost of capital?

It is again helpful to address this question by considering the benchmark situation where contracts are costlessly enforceable. It is then possible to have all payments at date 1 so that the insurance component can be separated from the financial market component in the usual way. The loss can again be represented by the random variable L with mean EL but now the residual risk that cannot be pooled away has variance σ_L^2 per policyholder. Equityholders in the insurance company will be needed to ensure that the residual risk that remains after pooling is covered. Initially, it is assumed they have unlimited liability or the funds they commit at date 0 are sufficient to cover the highest realization of the residual risk. This is again like the Lloyd's-type system in Section 4. As there, suppose there is a price Θ per unit of variance at date 1. The date 1 payment in this case for policyholders who do not suffer a loss will be

$$p_1 = EL + \Theta\sigma_L^2 \tag{15}$$

rather than $p_1 = EL$. Those policyholders that do suffer a loss will receive $L - (EL + \Theta\sigma_L^2)$ rather than L - EL.

The next step is to suppose that premiums are collected at date 0. In this case the analysis will be the same as above but with $EL + \Theta\sigma_L^2$ replacing EL. It will be assumed initially that there are perfect capital markets so all premiums are invested in the risk free asset. The date 0 premium will be

$$p_0 = \frac{EL + \Theta \sigma_L^2}{1 + r_F}. \tag{16}$$

The cost of capital (i.e. the rate for discounting the expected liabilities) alone will be the value of γ such that

$$\frac{EL}{1 + \gamma} = \frac{EL + \Theta \sigma_L^2}{1 + r_F}. \tag{17}$$

For different divisions the residual risk born by equityholders will differ and so σ_L^2 and hence the cost of capital will differ across divisions as in the previous section.

In the case where there are capital market imperfections and policyholders do not hold a sufficient amount of the risk free asset to offset the premium but instead hold a portfolio of risky assets, insurance companies will offer a range of policies depending on the clientele that is sought. Suppose that the portfolio the premiums are invested in has expected rate of return ER*, and its returns are independent of the insurance losses then the expected cost of insurance is

$$c_0 = \frac{EL}{1 + ER^*} + \frac{\Theta \sigma_L^2}{1 + r_F}. \tag{18}$$

The corresponding cost of capital is the value of γ such that

$$\frac{EL}{1 + \gamma} = \frac{EL}{1 + ER^*} + \frac{\Theta \sigma_L^2}{1 + r_F}. \tag{19}$$

Again there will be multiple costs of capital within each division. Across divisions σ_L^2 will vary so for a given value of ER* the cost of capital will also differ.

If portfolio returns and aggregate losses are correlated there will be an extra term in (18) to account for this. When losses are positively correlated with returns the expected cost will be higher than in (18) but when they are negatively correlated it will be lower.

As far as the premium is concerned, this will depend on the value of R_1 as before and the amount of residual financial risk that is optimal. If there is to be no residual financial risk then the premium must be sufficient to cover all liabilities and payments to the equityholders, as in Section 3, so

$$p_0 \; = \; \frac{EL}{1 \, + \, ER_1} \; + \; \frac{\Theta \, \sigma_L^2}{1 \, + \, r_F} \, .$$

(20)

If $1+R_1 = 0$ or is small then it will not be possible to have a guaranteeing premium and in addition to the residual risk from the insurance, there may also be residual risk from the investment of the premium. In this case the average cost of the insurance will be

$$c_0 \; = \; \frac{EL}{1 \, + \, ER^*} \; + \; \frac{\Theta \, \sigma_L^2 \, + \, \mu \, + \, \Theta \, \sigma^2}{1 \, + \, r_F}$$

(21)

and the premium will depend on the amount of residual financial risk that is optimal.

An assumption of the analysis above is that equityholders either have unlimited liability or the funds that they pledge at date 0 are sufficient to cover the highest realization of the residual risk. If this is not the case there is a real possibility of bankruptcy of the insurance company. There is then another residual holder, namely the fund which in most states guarantees the liabilities of insurance companies. This extra level of risk bearing could be added to the analysis. The precise way in which premiums and the cost of insurance will be affected depends on how the guarantee is implemented.

7. Taxes

An important assumption in the derivation of the Insurance Modigliani and Miller theorem is that there are no taxes. The introduction of taxes adds a number of dimensions to the analysis. If there is a difference between the way in which investment income is taxed when the investments are held directly and when they are held by the insurance company the Insurance Modigliani and Miller theorem will no longer hold. Typically, insurance companies are taxed less heavily in this respect than individuals and there may be opportunities for tax arbitrage. In this case, premiums will be higher than they need to be for pure insurance purposes to increase the investment component. Once again policies will be tailored to clienteles, but here the important thing will be tax status rather than the investors' optimal portfolios. In a competitive insurance market, it will be policyholders who obtain the benefits from the tax avoidance opportunities provided by insurance policies.

The main impact in terms of the effect on premiums and the cost of capital will be the fact that investment income and residual risk premia will be taxed. To illustrate, consider the case where capital markets are perfect, premiums are invested in the risk free asset and there is some residual risk from the liabilities. Here the counterpart of (16) if equityholders are to receive $\Theta\sigma^2$ after corporate taxes at date 1 is

$$p_0 = \frac{EL + \dfrac{\Theta\sigma_L^2}{1-t}}{1 + (1-t)r_F} \tag{22}$$

where t is the tax rate on insurance companies' income. The after-tax cost of capital will, similarly to (17), be the value of γ such that

$$\frac{EL}{1+\gamma} = \frac{EL + \dfrac{\Theta\sigma_L^2}{1-t}}{1 + (1-t)r_F}. \tag{23}$$

As before σ_L^2 will vary across divisions and so the divisional cost of capital will differ. Other cases can be similarly analyzed.

8. Conclusions

Traditional financial analyses of the divisional cost of capital which take the structure of the insurance firm as given have not adequately dealt with the issue of how to allocate the earnings from surplus to different divisions. This paper starts with the benchmark case where contracts are fully enforceable. This allows the insurance market component of companies' activities to be separated from the financial market component and leads to the notion of there being a market for residual risk. It is the price of residual risk and the amount of residual risk in each division that determines the compensation insurance companies' equityholders receive. As a result the allocation of earnings from a firm's surplus to the various divisions does not arise and it is possible to calculate a divisional cost of capital.

One important issue that does arise is how the scheme for estimating the divisional cost of capital described here could be implemented in practice. The main problem in this respect is finding an empirical estimate for the price of residual risk. This could be done in two ways. First of all data from markets where residual risk is directly guaranteed such as Lloyd's of London could be used. Alternatively, the excess premium earned by insurance company equityholders could be estimated and compared with the residual risk that they bear. Once the price of the residual risk has been found, using it to estimate the divisional cost of capital is relatively straightforward.

APPENDIX

The Market for Residual Risk

Consider a simple case where an investor has wealth W_1 at date 1 and von Neumann Morgenstern utility function $U(W_1)$. The person's coefficient of absolute risk aversion is defined to be

$$a(W) = -\frac{U''(W)}{U'(W)}. \qquad (A1)$$

Suppose the residual risk ε is normally distributed with mean $E\varepsilon$ and variance σ_ε^2. If the investor assumes a part of the residual risk $X\varepsilon$, then he or she receives an amount $X(E\varepsilon + \Theta\sigma_\varepsilon^2)$ at date 1 in return. The person's expected utility is

$$EU = EU[W_1 - X\varepsilon + X(E\varepsilon + \Theta\sigma_\varepsilon^2)]. \qquad (A2)$$

Using a Taylor's series expansion it can straightforwardly be shown[8] that for small $X\varepsilon$ this can be written in the form

$$EU \approx U(W_1 - 0.5aX^2\Theta_\varepsilon^2 + X\Theta\sigma_\varepsilon^2). \qquad (A3)$$

Choosing X to maximize this gives the demand for residual risk as

$$X \approx \frac{\Theta}{a}. \qquad (A4)$$

As might be expected intuitively, the less risk averse the person and the higher the price, the greater is the demand to bear the residual risk.

The price of residual risk Θ will be determined by the total demand for bearing it from individuals and the total supply of residual risk from insurance companies.

When the risk borne by each person is large, (A3) will no longer hold and it will be necessary to use more terms in the Taylor's series expansion. The risk premium individuals require to bear the residual risk will then depend on the third and higher moments of ε as well as the mean and the variance.

---

[8] See Pratt (1964).

REFERENCES

Allen, F. and D. Gale (1991). "Limited Market Participation and Volatility of Asset Prices," Rodney L. White Center Working Paper 2-92, University of Pennsylvania.

Biger, N. and Y. Kahane (1978). "Risk Considerations in Insurance Ratemaking," *Journal of Risk and Insurance* 45, 121-132.

Blume, M., J. Crockett and I. Friend (1974). "Stock Ownership in the United States: Characteristics and Trends," *Survey of Current Business*, 16-40.

Blume, M. and I. Friend (1978). *The Changing Role of the Individual Investor: A Twentieth Century Fund Report*, New York: Wiley.

Cooper, R. W. (1974). *Investment Return and Property-Liability Insurance Ratemaking* (Philadelphia: S.S. Huebner Foundation, University of Pennsylvania).

Cummins, J. D. (1990a). "Asset Pricing Models and Insurance Ratemaking," *Astin Bulletin* 20, 125-166.

Cummins, J. D. (1990b). "Financial Pricing of Property and Liability Insurance," working paper, University of Pennsylvania.

Cummins, J. D. (1990c). "Multi-Period Discounted Cash Flow Ratemaking Models in Property-Liability Insurance," *Journal of Risk and Insurance* 57, 79-109.

Cummins, J. D. and L. Chang (1983). "An Analysis of the New Jersey Formula for Including Investment Income in Property-Liability Insurance Ratemaking," *Journal of Insurance Regulation* 1, 555-573.

D'Arcy, S. and N. A. Doherty (1988). *Financial Theory of Insurance Pricing* (Philadelphia: S.S. Huebner Foundation, University of Pennsylvania).

Fairley, W. (1979). "Investment Income and Profit Margins in Property-Liability Insurance," *Bell Journal of Economics* 10, 192-210.

Ferrari, J. R. (1968). "A Note on the Basic Relationship of Underwriting, Investments, Leverage and Exposure to Total Return on Owners' Equity," *Proceedings of the Casualty Actuarial Society* 55, 295-302.

Hill, R. (1979). "Profit Regulation in Property Liability Insurance," *Bell Journal of Economics* 10, 172-191.

Modigliani, F. and M. H. Miller (1958). "The Cost of Capital, Corporation Finance, and the Theory of Investment," *American Economic Review* 48, 261-297.

Myers, S. and R. Cohn (1987). "Insurance Rate Regulation and the Capital Asset Pricing Model," in J. D. Cummins and S. E.

Harrington, eds., *Fair Rate of Return in Property-Liability Insurance* (Norwell, MA: Kluwer Academic Publishers).

National Council on Compensation Insurance, (1987). *The Impact of the Tax Reform Act of 1986 on Property-Liability Insurance Profits* (New York: The Council).

Pratt, J. W. (1964). "Risk Aversion in the Small and in the Large," *Econometrica* 32, 122-136.

Sharpe, W. F. (1970). *Portfolio Theory and Capital Markets* (New York: McGraw Hill).

7 CORPORATE RISK MANAGEMENT AND THE INSURANCE INDUSTRY

Clifford W. Smith, Jr.

Clarey Professor of Finance
W.E. Simon Graduate School
of Business Administration
University of Rochester

1. Introduction

There are at least two reasons that corporate risk management is important for firms in the insurance industry: (1) An insurance company's value depends directly on its risk-management policy. (2) The asset risk in an insurance company's loan portfolio depends on its customers' risk-management policies. In this paper, I analyze these implications of corporate risk-management for life insurance companies. In section 2, I suggest that corporate risks can be arrayed along a spectrum. At one extreme are firm-specific risks while at the other are market-wide risks. I note that forwards, futures, options, and swaps are

I would like to thank David Mayers and Charles W. Smithson for many stimulating conversations in the process of working on related questions. Financial support was provided by the John M. Olin Foundation and the Bradley Research Center of the University of Rochester.

specialized risk-management tools that allow the firm to hedge many sources of market-wide financial risk. In addition to these off-balance-sheet hedging alternatives, financially engineered instruments, such as dual-currency bonds, provide on-balance-sheet hedging alternatives. In section 3, I focus on motives for value-maximizing firms to purchase such specialized risk-management instruments. This section thus identifies the implications of hedging by customers for the insurer's asset portfolio risk. Section 4 examines the implications of life insurer risk-management policies. In section 5, I present my conclusions.

2. The Corporate Risk Spectrum

Firms are exposed to a wide variety of risks. Some of these risks are firm-specific risks; examples include fires, lawsuits, outcomes of research and development projects, and outcomes of exploration and development activities. Other risks are market-wide risks; examples include the impact of unexpected changes in interest rates, foreign exchange rates, oil prices and GNP. In figure 1, I array these risks along a risk spectrum. At one end are purely firm-specific risks and at the other are market-wide risks.

Corporate Risk Exposures

To analyze firms hedging incentives, it is important to understand how firm value is affected by individual risk exposures. For some risks, this relation is straightforward: For example an uninsured casualty loss directly reduces firm value. Other exposures are more complex. In figure 2, I illustrate the risk profile for an oil producer: higher oil prices, $\Delta P_{oil} > O$, raise revenues and increase firm value, $\Delta V > O$ (see Smith/Smithson/Wilford, 1990). Thus the risk profile has a positive slope (for simplicity, I draw a straight line). Note that for an oil user, the risk profile has a negative slope: In figure 2, higher oil prices ($\Delta P_{oil} > O$) raise costs and reduce firm value ($\Delta V < O$).

We can now examine the impact on firm value of hedging an exposure. For the oil user in figure 2 to hedge its exposure to oil prices, the firm must employ a hedging instrument that will appreciate in value ($\Delta V_{Hedge} > O$) with higher oil prices ($\Delta P_{oil} > O$). Hedging reduces the firm's exposure to oil-price changes because gains on the hedge offset losses in

FIGURE 1
Risk Management Spectrum

Risk Exposures	Risk Management Tools		
	Off-Balance-Sheet	On-Balance Sheet	
		Financial	Production
Firm Specific Fire	Insurance		Loss Prevention
Lawsuit	Warrants		
Payoffs to R&D Projects		Convertible Bonds	Joint Ventures
Commodity Prices	Forwards	Hybrids (Dual Currency Oil Indexed Notes, etc.)	Technology Choice
Interest Rates	Futures		Plant Siting
	Swaps		
Market Wide Foreign Exchange Rates	Options		Vertical Integration

the firm's core business. This impact of risk management reduces the variance of the firm-value distribution.

Off-Balance-Sheet Hedging Instruments.

I believe that a major benefit of arranging the sources of risks in this risk spectrum is that different risks are hedged through different hedging instruments. In the second column of figure 1, I note that firm-specific risks like fires or lawsuits can be hedged through insurance policies. While firms can change production or financing policies to hedge exposures ("on-balance-sheet" hedging), financial risks can also be managed with the use of off-balance-sheet instruments. Market-wide

FIGURE 2
Relation Between the Change In Firm Value and Change In
Oil Prices for an Oil Producer and an Oil User

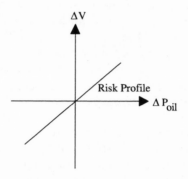

For an oil Producer, rising oil prices ($\Delta P_{oil} > 0$) and rising revenues
lead to an increase in the value of the firm ($\Delta V > 0$).

(a)

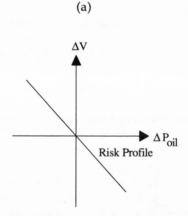

For an oil user, rising oil prices ($\Delta P_{oil} > 0$) mean increasing costs so the
value of the firm declines ($\Delta V < 0$).

(b)

risks such as interest rates, foreign-exchange rates, and commodity prices can be hedged through forward, futures, swap, and option contracts. In discussing these instruments, I want to focus on the fact that these are four interrelated instruments that allow the firm's managers to hedge financial risks.

- **Forward Contracts.** Of these four basic off-balance-sheet hedging instruments, the forward contract is the simplest. A forward contract obligates it's owner to buy a stipulated asset on a stipulated date at a stipulated price; these provisions are all specified at contract origination. At the stipulated date, if the spot market price of the asset is higher than the stipulated price (the exercise price) then the buyer has a valuable contract. Its value is equal to the difference between the exercise price and the market value of the asset. However, the market price is lower than the exercise price, the buyer has suffered a loss. Figure 3 illustrates a foreign-exchange forward, an oil forward, and an interest-rate forward (forward rate agreement). In figure 4, the payoff profiles from buying a forward and from selling a forward contract are illustrated. Thus, if a firm's core-business cash flows are a negative function of the value of an asset, buying a forward contract hedges that exposure.

- **Future Contracts.** A futures contact is quite similar in form to a forward contract--buying a futures also obligates the purchaser to buy a stipulated asset at a stipulated price on a stipulated date. The substantive difference between forwards and futures involves contract administration. Specifically (1) forwards are generally over-the-counter instruments where futures are exclusively exchange-traded instruments; (2) over the life of the forward contract, all the value change is transferred at the expiration date, futures contracts are marked-to-market daily thus the value change is transferred daily; (3) futures markets require that buyers and sellers post a performance bond called "margin (if the value of a futures contract increase over the day, the margin account is credited; if it falls, the account is

FIGURE 3
Illustration of Cash Flows From (a) a Foreign-Exchange Forward,
(b) an Oil Producer, and (c) an Interest-rate Forward Contract

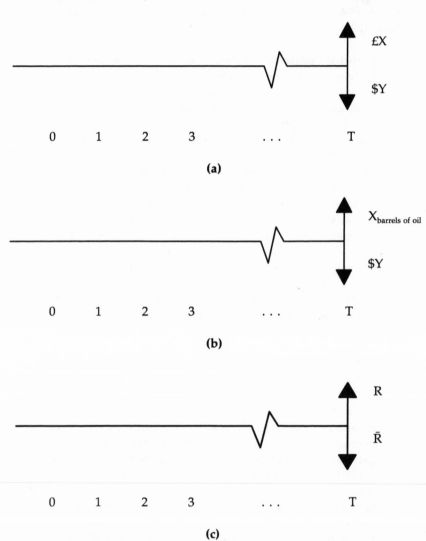

(a)

(b)

(c)

FIGURE 4
Payoff Profile From (a) Buying a Forward and
(b) Selling a Forward Contract

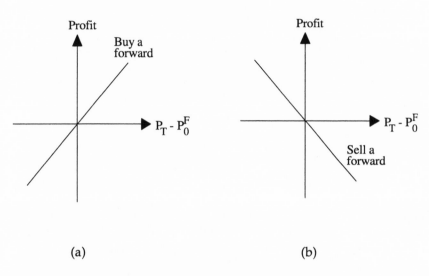

(a)   (b)

At contract maturity (time=T), the profit to the buyer of a forward contract is equal to the difference between the spot price at T and the exercise price agreed to at contract origination ($P_T - P_0^F$) times the size of the forward contract. The profit to the seller of the contract is the reverse.

debited); (4) in a forward the contract terms are customized while to facilitate a liquid secondary market in the futures, contracts are standardized with respect to assets, expiration dates, and contract sizes. In sum, although futures and forward contracts are administered in different ways, their impacts on hedging firm value are similar; in fact figure 4 can be applied to futures as well as forward contracts.

Swap Contracts. A swap is, in essence, a strip of forward contracts, each with a different maturity date,

FIGURE 5
Interest Rate Swap Cash Flows for
Party Paying Fixed and Receiving Floating

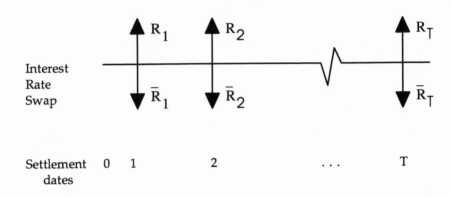

The party pays a series of cash flows determined by the T-period fixed interest rate ($\bar{R}_t$) at the origination in return for a series of cash flows (R_t) determined by the relevant floating interest rate.

(see Smith/Smithson/Wakeman (1986, 1988)). A swap obligates two parties to exchange cash flows at specified intervals. For example, in an interest-rate swap, parties exchange cash flows determined by two different interest rates. Figure 5 illustrates an interest-rate swap from the perspective of the party who is paying cash flows based on a fixed interest rate ($\bar{R}$) and receives cash flows based on a floating rate (R). At each settlement date, this interest-rate swap contains an imbedded forward contract on interest rates. Swaps have characteristics that place their behavior between that of forward and futures contracts: (1) swaps are typically over-the-counter, not exchange-traded contracts—in this respect they are more like forwards; (2) swaps distribute partial value changes periodically over the life of the contract rather than all at the expiration date--in this respect they are more like futures.

Options. An option gives the owner of the contract the right to transact, but not the obligation (see Black/Scholes (1973) or Smith (1976)). Options come in two basic forms: puts and calls. A call is an option to buy a stipulated asset at a stipulated price on or before a stipulated date; a put is an option to sell. Puts and calls can be both bought and written. In fact, buying a call plus writing a put on the same asset with the same exercise price and the same expiration date is equivalent to buying a forward. This equivalence among puts, calls, and forwards is referred to as put-call parity.

On-Balance-Sheet Hedging

The last ten years has witnessed a virtual explosion in the use of financially engineered securities. The financial community provides customized solutions to corporate clients' financing problems in much the same way General Motors provides customized solutions to their customers' transportation problems. Chevrolet offers several different models with different wheel bases, different engines, different exteriors, different interior appointments, different sound systems, etc. By exploiting the myriad of opportunities to mix different off-the-shelf options, Chevrolet can produce many different cars. Similarly, the financially engineered instruments are customized packages of cash-flow claims, but the components that make up the contracts are themselves fairly standard off-the-shelf instruments: loans, forwards, swaps, and options. (see Smith/Smithson (1990)). For example, Phillip Morris Credit Corporation recently issued over $50 million of dual-currency bonds. While the principal amount of the bonds is stated in US dollars, the interest payments are denominated in Swiss-Francs. Figure 6 illustrates how this dual-currency bond can be thought of as a financial package containing a level-coupon Swiss-Franc bond plus a long-term forward-exchange forward contract to exchange the Swiss-Franc principal repayment into dollars.

SallieMae, the Student Loan Marketing Association issued what

FIGURE 6
A Dual Currency Bond

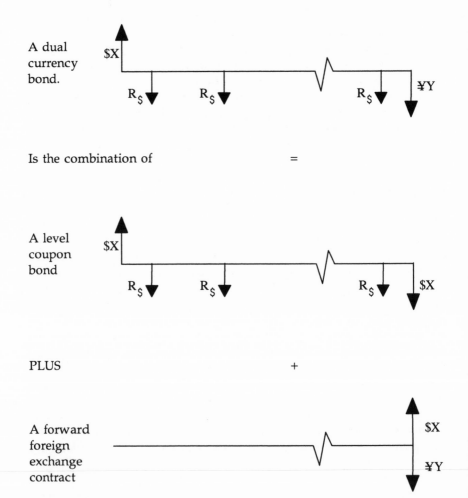

A dual
currency
bond.

Is the combination of   =

A level
coupon
bond

PLUS   +

A forward
foreign
exchange
contract

it called yield-curve notes. These notes specify that if interest rates fall by 100 basis points that the coupon payment on the notes rises. Figure 7 illustrates that this "reverse floating rate" bond can be thought of as a package containing a traditional fixed rate bond plus a swap where the party pays fixed and receives floating. The net coupon payments on the yield-curve notes are equal to twice the fixed rate minus the floating rate times the principal; thus, if the floating rate rises, the net coupon payment falls.

As a last example, the Standard Oil Company recently issued over $35 million in oil indexed notes. At maturity, the holder of each note receives $1000 plus the excess of the crude oil price over $25 multiplied by 170 barrels ($1000 + 170 x (Pcrude oil - $25)). These notes are thus equivalent to a 48 month maturity zero-coupon bond with a face value of $1000 plus a 4 year call option on 170 barrels of crude oil with an exercise price of $25.

3. The Benefits of Risk Management

Financial market volatility has increased dramatically over the past two decades. Given the corporation's risk exposure, increased volatility of foreign exchange rates, interest rates and commodity prices translates into increased volatility of firm value. Since risk management reduces firm-value volatility, one might presume that all firms would want to engage in hedging. Yet there is wide variation in the use of risk-management instruments across firms. Thus, I focus on understanding firm characteristics that provide strong economic incentives to hedge.

Company Ownership Structure

To examine economic risk-management incentives, I assume that the firms objective is to maximize the expected present value of its net cash flows:

$$V_j = \sum_{t=0}^{T} \frac{E(NCF_{jt})}{(1 + \bar{r}_{jt})^t} \tag{1}$$

where NCF_{jt} is firm j's net cash flow at time t and $\bar{r}_{jt}$ is the required rate of return for cash flows of this risk received at date t. Hence, a company

FIGURE 7
A Reverse Floating Rate Loan

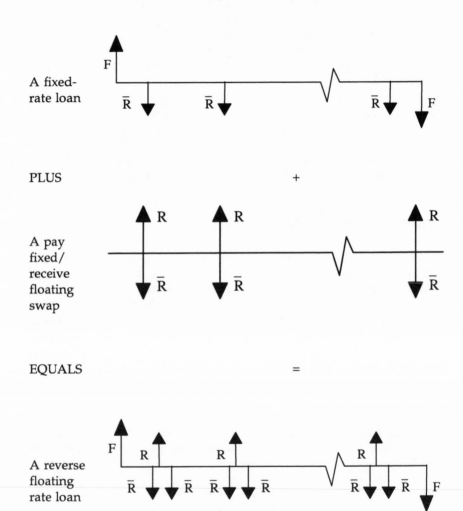

A fixed-
rate loan

PLUS   +

A pay
fixed/
receive
floating
swap

EQUALS   =

A reverse
floating
rate loan

should manage its financial price risk if that risk-management strategy increases its expected present value.

Individuals, because they are risk averse, have an incentive to hedge because reducing risk lowers the required rate of return on a risky project. However, for a widely held corporation, this logic fails. Portfolio theory tells us that the firm's required rate of return doesn't depend on total risk but only on systematic (non-diversifiable) risk. Since these hedging instruments work primarily on non-systematic risk, their use does not provide a lower discount rate for firms with well-diversified investors. However, for proprietorships, partnerships and closely-held firms, organizations where owners do not hold well-diversified portfolios, risk aversion can be an important risk-management incentive (see Mayers/Smith (1982)).

If, for widely-held firms, hedging does not reduce the firm's required rate of return, then for hedging to increase value it must increase the firm's expected net cash flows. To focus on how this might occur, it is useful to recall the Modigliani-Miller proposition. It states: If there are no taxes, no transactions costs, and if the firm's real investment activities are fixed, then the firm's financial decisions (including risk management decisions) will not affect firm value. Although this is how Modigliani/Miller stated the proposition in their original paper, it is useful to restate it: If financial decisions affect value, they must do so because of their impact on transactions costs, taxes, or investment decisions. We thus can employ the M and M proposition to identify which firms have strong economic incentives to hedge.

Taxes

As long as the firm faces a constant effective tax rate (the tax function is linear) hedging doesn't affect the firm's expected tax liability. But if the firm's tax function is convex (the firm faces some form of effective tax progressivity) then hedging taxable income reduces the volatility of pretax income and thus reduces the firm's expected tax liability; this is a direct implication of Jensen's Inequality (see Smith/Stulz (1985)). Convexity in the tax schedule can arise from three general considerations: (1) Although its range is limited, the tax code specifies statutory progressivity. (2) Tax-preference items (tax-loss carry forwards, foreign tax credits, investment tax credits, etc) generally have limitation on use; if taxable income falls below some level, the value of the tax preference item is reduced either by the loss of the tax shield or by the postponement of its use (see DeAngelo/Masulis (1980)), (3)   The alternative minimum tax specifies liabilities linked to the difference between financial (reported) and taxable income. Thus firms with stronger tax-related economic incentives to hedge are: (1) firms with a higher probability of income in the progressive region of the tax schedule (e.g. smaller firms, start-up firms).   (2)   firms with more tax-preference items, and (3) firms with more volatility in the difference between financial and taxable income.

Costs of Financial Distress

Financial risk-management reduces the probability of a company encountering financial distress by reducing the variance of firm value. Thus, risk management reduces the costs the firm would face if it met with financial distress. The magnitude of the cost reduction depends on (1) the change in probability of distress from hedging and (2) the level of costs imposed by financial distress.

Costs of financial distress can be decomposed into two major components: (1) the direct legal expenses of dealing with a default, bankruptcy, reorganization, or liquidation and (2) the indirect costs because of the modified incentives of the firm's various claimholders. For example, if the firm files for bankruptcy and attempts to reorganize its business, the bankruptcy court judge overseeing the case is unlikely to approve non-routine expenditures--he gets little credit if they turn out well but is blamed by creditors with impaired claims if they turn out badly.   Thus firms in bankruptcy are likely to systematically pass up positive net present value projects because of the bankruptcy court's oversight.

Firm's that avoid bankruptcy also face incentives to turn down positive net present value projects.   With fixed claims in its capital structure a firm can encounter circumstances where the benefits of taking a positive net present value project accrue to the debtholders (Myers (1977)).   The greater firm's leverage, the greater this underinvestment incentive.   In figure 8, I illustrate this incentive to engage in risk management. The risk profile of the an oil user indicates that if oil prices increase, firm value falls. Given the fixed claims in the firm's capital structure, leverage increases.   Higher leverage exacerbates the underinvestment problem and the firm turns down additional positive

FIGURE 8
Illustration of the Underinvestment Costs for Oil User

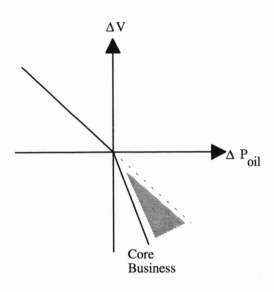

net present value projects. Thus, the underinvestment costs are graphically illustrated by the shaded area in figure 8. For this firm to hedge its oil price exposure it buys oil forwards, futures, or swaps--it adds a hedging instrument with payoffs that increase with higher oil prices (see figure 9). The firms net exposure to oil price changes has been reduced; with the hedge, a given increase in oil prices results in a smaller fall in firm value, a smaller induced change in leverage, a smaller exacerbation of the underinvestment problem, and a reduction in the frequency of rejected positive net present value projects (see Mayers/Smith (1987)). Thus, the impact of hedging on the control of the underinvestment problem is graphically illustrated by the difference in the shaded area between the firms core business exposure in figure 8 and its net exposure in figure 9.

FIGURE 9
Impact of Hedging

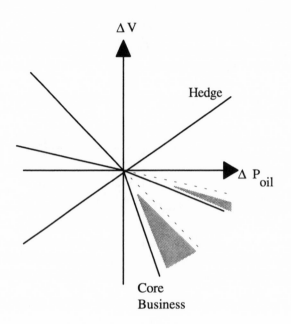

Riskshifting within the Corporation

While thus far I have focused on corporate bondholders and stockholders, the firm is really a vast network of contracts among parties with common as well as conflicting interests. Certain claimholders in the corporation differ from stockholders and bondholders in an important dimension--managers, employees, and certain customers and suppliers are generally less able to diversify their claims on the firm. Thus, (like the owners of a closely-held firm) these claimholders' risk aversion can motivate corporate risk-management activities.

To understand the risk-management incentives of corporate managers and employees, it is important to examine their compensation package and its specification of the payoff structure of their claims on their firm. For a manager or employee primarily compensated through salary, their risk aversion will motivate lobbying for extensive risk-management activities. But a manager compensated through extensive use of stock options or bonus plans can have incentives to increase the volatility of reported earnings or stock prices because of the option-like payoffs of the compensation provisions (see Smith/Watts (1982)). The extent of these incentives depend both on the relative importance of the use of various components in the compensation package but also on the degree to which a specific component is either in or out of the money.

Financial distress can impose large costs on firms that produce products where quality is difficult to ascertain prior to purchase (e.g., airlines). Financial distress by such a firm can change the customers' expectations of product quality and thus their demand prices. These problems are ultimately related to the underinvestment problems discussed above. For example, if an airline gets into financial distress, the benefits of an investment in maintaining the airplane disproportionately accrue to the fixed claimholders. Customers thus rationally expect that the firms will reduce its maintenance activities. Therefore, such firms have incentives to pre-position themselves so that they are less exposed to these risks--in general they will employ less leverage and engage in more hedging than an otherwise similar firm.

The more important are product warranties or guarantees offered to the customers, the larger are the costs of financial distress. Product warranties are like product-specific insurance policies. If the firm gets into financial distress, the value of this insurance policy falls, revenue falls, and financial distress problems are exacerbated. Note that similar problems arise where there is an important continuing stream of firm-provided customer services by the firm; for example, replacement parts for automobiles or continuing software development by a computer manufacturer.

A complimentary set of problems arise between the firm and its suppliers. These problems are most severe when the supplier provides specialized inputs to the firm especially where there is a relatively long time between incurring production costs and the ultimate receipt of the revenue. Financial distress in such circumstances disrupts normal supply relation-ships. Frequently the supplier will demand either cash in advance or on delivery, exacerbating the firm's liquidity problems. These change in effective supply prices are additional costs of financial distress.

4. Implications for Insurers

In section 3, I focus on the risk management implications for the management of the insurer's private placement loan customers. In this section, I turn to the risk management policy for the insurance company itself. Life insurance is a specific industry where product quality is an important concern of potential customers. This concern is primarily focused on whether the financial commitments of the insurer under the contract will be met. Thus, risk management by firms in the industry affect the probability of financial distress and therefore the premiums potential customers are willing to pay. While for specific insurers other risks are important, in this analysis I will focus primarily on interest-rate exposure management.

Insurer Exposure to Interest Rates

If the effective maturity of an insurer's asset portfolio (duration) is greater than to the effective maturity on its book of liabilities, then the insurer is exposed to interest rate risk. If interest rates rise unexpectedly the market value of the insurer falls--the market value of its asset portfolio will experience larger capital losses than that of its liabilities. Absent imbedded options in its financial contracts, the response of value to unexpected changes in interest rates is generally symmetric. If interest rates fall unexpectedly, the firm value rises. Figure 10 illustrates the effect of interest rate changes on the value of an insurer that markets shorter term insurance policies and invests in longer-term fixed rate mortgage loans: higher interest rates ($\Delta R > O$) lower firm value ($\Delta V < O$). With no imbedded options in the loan or insurance contracts, the slope of the exposure profile is:

$$\frac{dV}{dR} = \frac{[L * D(L) - A * D(A)]}{1 + R} \qquad (2)$$

Where L is the market value of liabilities,
A is the market value of assets,
D(L) is the duration of liabilities,
D(A) is the duration of assets,
R is the market interest rate.

FIGURE 10
Line aa Represents the Interest-rate Exposure for a Life Insurer With a Duration Imbalance But No Imbedded Interest-rate Options. Line bb Represents the Interest-rate Exposure of a Life Insurer With Imbedded Interest-rate Options Sold to its Insurance and Loan Customers

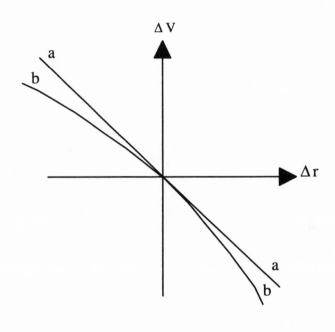

Line aa in figure 10 depicts equation (2) for such an insurer. If the duration imbalance (L*D(L)) - A*D(A)) is reduced, the response of value to a change in interest rates, dV/dR, falls and the line becomes flatter. Conversely, if the duration imbalance increases, line aa becomes a steeper and the sensitivity of value to interest rates increases.

Effect of Imbedded Options

        Insurers historically have offered loan contracts which have given
customers the option to prepay the loan prior to maturity. Life insurance
contracts frequently include imbedded options (see Smith (1982)). For
example, whole-life policies traditionally contain a policy-loan option; this
option provides a guaranteed line of credit for the insured and typically
specifies a maximum interest rate on the borrowed funds. Thus, if
market interest rates rise, these policy-loan options increase in value.
Also, contracts frequently contain an option to purchase additional
insurance at guaranteed rates. Such options are more valuable if market
interest rates fall. These exposures are exacerbated by some of the
prepayment or redemption options embedded in newer instruments such
as single premium deferred annuities (SPDAs) and guaranteed
investment contracts (GICs)
        Exercise of these imbedded interest rate options by policyholders
or borrowers present an important complication to the analysis of the
effects of interest-rate changes on insurer value. Since the life insurance
company has written the imbedded options sold both to the policyholders
and the borrowers, line aa in figure 10 is not appropriate if interest rates
change. If interest rates fall, policyholders have incentives to exercise
their option to take out additional coverage at guaranteed rates and
borrowers have incentives to prepay existing mortgages. In many cases
they refinance the property at the then prevailing interest rate. Mortgage
prepayments thus have two effects on the value of a short-funded
insurer: (1) When the mortgage is prepaid, the lender loses a capital gain
equal to the difference between the market and book value of the
mortgage. (2) The lender must reinvest the cash in some new financial
instrument which yields the now prevailing lower rate of interest. If
mortgage contracts allow prepayment, the mortgage lender receives
capital gains only on the mortgages which are not prepaid. Line bb to
the left of the origin in figure 10 represents these capital gains.
Prepayments reduce the response of the value of the insurer to interest-
rate reductions. This effect is reinforced by the policyholders exercise of
options to increase coverage at guaranteed rates. Since policy-loan
options are more valuable at higher rates, line aa also overstates the
change in firm value if interest rates rise. With higher rates, customers
will exercise their policy-loan options, taking out loans at below-market
rates. The value of this option is shown in line bb to the right of the

origin

Because of these imbedded options offered in both insurance and loan contracts, value changes produced by interest-rate changes are not symmetric. Increases in rates lead to reductions in loan prepayments and a lengthening of the effective maturity of the loan portfolio. This increases the fall in the value of an insurance company from a rate rise. At the same time, policyholders reduce their demand for optional fixed-price insurance but increase their demand for fixed-rate policy loans, again increasing the fall in the value of the insurer. These imbedded financial options cause the gains from declines in interest rates to be less than the losses associated with rate increases. As a result, expected insurer value is reduced by increases in interest-rate volatility.

Hedging Insurer Interest-Rate Exposure

The insurer can change the slope of its exposure with simple static portfolio strategies involving forwards, futures or swaps. For example, by entering an interest-rate swap where the insurer pays fixed and receives floating, its exposure to interest rates can be reduced. In fig. 11 line b'b' represents the firm's net exposure to interest-rate changes after hedging. However the firm is still exposed to changes in interest-rate volatility. In essence, the firm has written a set of imbedded interest-rate options to its customers; thus it is short interest-rate volatility. Unexpected increases in volatility reduce firm value while unexpected reductions in volatility increase firm value.

The firm on hedge this risk by buying interest-rate options. The options can be purchased by themselves or imbedded in other financial packages (for example CMO residuals). But a strategy of hedging the portfolio of imbedded interest-rate options written by a major insurer through buying a matching portfolio of options is a unwieldy and expensive proposition. It is likely to be more efficient to manage this risk through a dynamic hedging strategy.

In general, one cannot hedge both the interest-rate risk and the volatility risk through the simple dynamic trading strategy pioneered by Black/Scholes. Given Black/Scholes assumptions of (1) constant volatility of the underlying asset, (2) no jumps in the value of the underlying asset, and (3) continuous costless trading, the only risk that must be hedged is that associated with unexpected changes in the underlying asset value. They note that the value of an option will have a specified sensitivity to

FIGURE 11
Illustration of the Impact of Hedging Interest-rate
Risk With Swap for Life Insurer in Figure 10

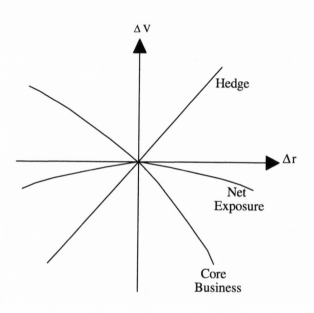

changes in the value of its underlying asset; this is the delta of the option. Their delta-hedging strategy replicates the option payoffs by acquiring rate-sensitive assets as rates rise (as the option goes in the money). While this dynamic delta-hedging strategy can hedge the firm's interest-rate risk, given the volatility of rates, it generally cannot also hedge volatility risk. To dynamically manage this risk, one must extend the basic principle to hedge additional option parameters.

In addition to the option's delta, a sophisticated dynamic hedging strategy must consider the option's gamma and vega. Gamma is the change in delta associated with a change in the underlying asset value (thus gamma is the second derivative of the option value with respect to change in the underlying asset value). Vega (also called Kappa) is the sensitivity of the value of the option to changes in the volatility of the underlying asset. One generally requires at least three rate-sensitive assets to simultaneously hedge the option's delta, gamma, and vega (see Bookstabler (1991)). With three linearly independent rate-sensitive assets, portfolio weights for the hedging portfolio can be derived. With such an enhanced option replication strategy (the term used by Kidder, Peabody), the valuation errors firm periodic rather than continuous rebalancing, jumps in the underlying asset value, and volatility changes are reduced.

With more than three assets one can employ programming techniques to identify the minimum-cost enhanced option replication strategy. However, there are several potential pitfalls in implementing such a technique. The relevant parameters must estimated; this estimation process inevitably involves measurement error. Employing more assets than identified as "optimal" can reduce the impact of measurement error induced selection bias. One must be careful if the program identifies out-of-the-money options; such options are typically illiquid.

5. Conclusions

Insurance firms have long exploited certain risk-management activities (1) the industry has been based on the risk-reduction benefits of diversification; and (2) reinsurance contracts control financial implications of extreme observations from the loss distribution. However, the control of financial risks via forwards, futures, swaps and options has been less extensively pursued. Based on his survey, Hoyt(1989) concludes that there is a problem, especially among smaller insurance companies, with hiring and retaining management with the requisite skills to manage a financial risk-management program.

However, if financial prices remain volatile, the implications of not hedging can prove disastrous. Moreover, with the increased awareness of the financial-distress problems on the part of both regulatory bodies and policyholders as a result of the Executive Life, case the pressure for adoption effective risk-management policies by insurers is likely to mount.

In this paper, two major implications of risk management theory for life insurers are explored: (1) The impact of interest rate risk management policy on the value of a life insurance company, and (2) the risk management policies of loan customers for the risk of the insurer's

asset portfolio.   With respect to the first issue I argue that in the
traditional way this business is structured, the insurer sells imbedded
interest rate options and thus creates a significant exposure to interest-
rate volatility. This exposure can be managed only by buying options.
The second issue is important specifically because insurers have not
aggressively pressed their private-placement loan customers about their
hedging policies.   A review of the arguments offered in this paper
indicates that hedging by lenders is not a substitute for hedging by
borrowers.   The motives identified above change corporate activities,
cash-flow distributions, and firm value. The benefits cannot be generated
without borrower participation.

REFERENCES

Black, Fischer and Myron Scholes (1973) "The Pricing of Options and Corporate Liabilities," *Journal of Political Economy* 81, 637-659.

Hoyt, Robert E., (1989). "The Use of Financial Futures by Life Insurers," *Journal of Risk and Insurance*, December 1989, Volume LVI, No. 4.

Mayers, David and Clifford W. Smith (1982) "On the Corporate Demand for Insurance," *Journal of Business* 55, No. 2, 281-296.

Mayers, David and Clifford W. Smith (1987) "Corporate Insurance and the Underinvestment Problem," *Journal of Risk and Insurance*, Vol. LIV, No. 1, 45-54.

Myers, Stewart (1977) "Determinants of Corporate Borrowing," *Journal of Financial Economics* 5, No. 2, 145-175.

Nance, Deana and Clifford W. Smith, and Charles W. Smithson (1993) "On the Determinants of Corporate Hedging," *Journal of Finance* (forthcoming).

Smith, Clifford W. (1976), "Option Pricing: A Review," *Journal of Financial Economics*, Vol. 3, 3-52.

Smith, Clifford W, and Charles W. Smithson, "Handbook of Financial Engineering," (Harper and Row: New York) (1990).

Smith, Clifford W., Charles W. Smithson and Lee M. Wakeman, "The Market for Interest Rate Swaps," *Financial Management* Vol. 17, No. 4, 34-44 (Winter 1988).

Smith, Clifford W. and René Stulz (1985), "The Determinants of Firm's Hedging Policies," *Journal of Financial and Quantitative Analysis* 20, No. 4, 391-405.

Smith, Clifford W. and Ross Watts (1982), "Incentive and Tax Effects of U.S. Executive Compensation Plans," *Australian Journal of Management* 7, 139-157.

Smith, Clifford W., Charles W. Smithson and Sykes D. Wilford, "Financial Risk Management," (Ballinger/Institutional Investor: New York) (1990).

Smith, Michael (1982) :Life Insurance Policy as an Options Package," *Journal of Risk and Insurance* 49, 583-601.

8 ASSET/LIABILITY MANAGEMENT: FROM IMMUNIZATION TO OPTION-PRICING THEORY

Elias S.W. Shiu

Principal Financial Group Professor
University of Iowa

Introduction

It was nearly forty years ago when the eminent British actuary F.M. Redington published the paper "Review of the Principles of Life-Office Valuations," in which he suggested the principle that there should be equal and parallel treatment in the valuation of assets and liabilities. His theory of immunization for insulating a portfolio against interest rate fluctuations follows as an immediate consequence of this principle. A deficiency in Redington's model is the assumption that the asset and liability cash flows are fixed and certain. In this paper we show that his theory can be extended to the general case of interest-sensitive cash flows (SPDA, UL, MBS, etc.) by means of modern option-pricing theory.

Support from the Natural Sciences and Engineering Research Council of Canada is gratefully acknowledged.

1. Interest Rate Risk

A major problem facing the insurance industry is that of interest rate fluctuations. The term C-3 risk was coined by the distinguished actuary C.L. Trowbridge, when he was Chairman of the Society of Actuaries Committee on Valuation and Related Matters, to denote the risk of losses due to changes in interest rates - changes in either the level of interest rates or the shape of the yield curve. The letter "C" stands for contingency. Trowbridge used the term C-1 risk to denote the risk of asset defaults and decreases in market values of equity investments, and the term C-2 risk to denote mortality and morbidity risks - the risk of losses from increases in claims and from pricing deficiencies, other than those from C-1 and C-3 risks. Subsequently, the term C-4 risk was also used, denoting accounting, managerial, social and regulatory risks.

To understand what C-3 risk or interest rate risk means, consider a block of insurance business and its associated assets. The *asset cash flow* in any future time period is defined as the investment income and capital maturities expected to occur in that time period. The *liability cash flow* (or *insurance cash flow*) in any future time period is defined as the sum of the policy claims, policy surrenders and expenses minus the premium income expected to occur in that time period. The *net cash flow* is defined as the difference between the asset cash flow and liability cash flow. A positive net cash flow means that the asset cash flow exceeds the liability cash flow, generating excess cash for (re)investment. Losses may occur, if interest rates are below the current level when the net cash flows are positive. On the other hand, negative net cash flows mean cash shortages for meeting liability obligations. At such times it would involve the liquidation of assets or borrowing within the company. Losses may occur, if interest rates are above the current level when the net cash flows are negative.

The C-3 risk problem is further aggravated by the various options embedded in the assets and liabilities, i.e., the asset and liability cash flows are functions of interest rates. When interest rates go up, policyholders are more likely to surrender their policies (so as to reinvest the cash values elsewhere for higher return) or exercise their policy loan options. On the other hand, when interest rates fall, bonds are more likely to be called and mortgages may be prepaid earlier than expected.

2. Cash-Flow Matching and Immunization

Two useful methods for insulating a fixed-income portfolio against shifts in the term structure of interest rates are *cash-flow matching* and *immunization*. Cash-flow matching or dedication was formally suggested by the mathematical economist Tjalling C. Koopmans (1942), when he was a Dutch refugee working for the Penn Mutual Life Insurance Company, for managing assets and liabilities in life insurance companies (Fisher, 1980, p. 22). Algorithms for cash-flow matching can be found in the papers by Hiller and Schaack (1990) and Kocherlakota, Rosenbloom and Shiu (1988, 1990). The problem is to determine the cheapest portfolio of fixed income securities such that, for all periods in the planning horizon, the accumulated net cash flows are nonnegative. It can be assumed in the model that, when there is excess cash to invest, the interest rate will be low, and that, when borrowing or asset liquidation is needed, the interest rate will be high. The key technique in cash-flow matching is the method of linear programming. (Together with Leonid V. Kantorovich, Koopmans was awarded the 1975 Nobel Memorial Prize in Economics for his independent discovery of linear programming and applications of linear programming to resource allocation problems.) It should be noted that cash-flow matching techniques normally require the cash flows to be fixed and certain.

The term *immunization* was coined in a 1952 paper entitled "Review of the Principles of Life-Office Valuations" by the eminent British actuary Frank M. Redington, who was Chief Actuary of Prudential Assurance. Note from the title that the theme of the paper was supposed to be on valuation rather than on strategies for matching assets and liabilities. In this historical paper, Redington suggested that actuaries should adopt "a similar basis for [the valuation of] both assets and liabilities." This was the first instance when the cardinal principle of valuation was laid down - that there should be equal and parallel treatment in the valuation of assets and liabilities. As a corollary to this principle, Redington derived his theory that, to immunize the surplus value of a block of business against interest rate fluctuations, one should equate the *mean term* of the assets to that of the liabilities while requiring the assets to be more spread out than the liabilities. Partly for this work, Redington was awarded a Gold Medal by the British Institute of Actuaries in 1968.

It turned out that Redington's concept of mean term already appeared in the work of Frederick R. Macaulay (1938), whose *duration* is the standard terminology today. Incidentally, Frederick Macaulay's father and grandfather were presidents of Sun Life of Canada. Two Nobel laureates in Economics, Sir John Hicks (1939) and Paul A. Samuelson (1945), had also independently come up with the concept of duration. For historical reviews on immunization theory and duration analysis, see Weil (1973), Fisher (1980), Hawawini (1982, pp. 1-30) and Bierwag, Kaufman and Toevs (1982). Several books which deal solely with immunization theory and duration analysis are Hawawini (1982), Kaufman, Bierwag and Toevs (1983), Granito (1984) and Bierwag (1987). Two important papers that introduced the concept of immunization to North American actuaries were Hickman (1971) and Vanderhoof (1972). It should be noted that some scholars (Hawawini, 1982, pp. 4-5) would argue that the concept of mean term or duration had been anticipated by another eminent British actuary George J. Lidstone (1893).

We next present a review of the classical immunization theory and then show how it can be extended to the general case of interest-sensitive cash flows by means of modern option-pricing theory.

3. Redington's Principle of Consistent Treatment of Assets and Liabilities

Consider a block of insurance business and its associated assets at time t = 0. For t ≥ 0, let A_t denote the asset cash flow expected to occur at time t, i.e., the interest income, dividends, rent, capital maturities, repayments and prepayments expected to occur at that time. Let L_t denote the liability cash flow (or insurance cash flow) expected to occur at time t, i.e., the policy claims, policy surrenders, policy loan payments, policyholder dividends, expenses and taxes, less premium income, less policy loan repayments, less policy loan interest expected at that time. For a given interest rate i, the asset and liability present values are given by the sums

$$\sum_t \frac{A_t}{(1 + i)^t},\qquad(3.1)$$

and

$$\sum_t \frac{L_t}{(1 + i)^t}, \tag{3.2}$$

respectively. Let S(i) denote the surplus of this block of business, evaluated at the interest rate i. As surplus is the difference between asset and liability values, we have

$$S(i) = \sum_t \frac{A_t}{(1 + i)^t} - \sum_t \frac{L_t}{(1 + i)^t}. \tag{3.3}$$

Let us pause to consider the historical significance of (3.3).

It was about 1800 when William Morgan of the Equitable Life Assurance Society (London) began to discuss valuation methods. "Morgan was the first actuary who could be called a professional actuary in the sense that the term is understood today. ... Outstanding among Morgan's string of actuarial 'firsts' were his setting up of a balance sheet to take account of a life insurance company's future liabilities and his appreciation of the significance of the results; his realization of the need to carry forward a margin of surplus to prevent the policyholder dividend system from breaking down; the classifying and measuring of the available sources of profit. ... Morgan was also the first in a long succession of actuaries to have trouble from policyholders and directors who refused to appreciate the need of holding adequate reserves for paying future claims instead of paying higher dividends." (Mitchell, 1974, pp. 6-7)

As Redington (1982, p. 86) pointed out, Morgan "would have been astonished to learn how little progress was to be made" on valuation theory for the next 150 years. Before the appearance of Redington's 1952 paper, it did not seem obvious to actuaries that there should be consistency of treatment in the valuation of assets and liabilities. In making a valuation, actuaries used to assume that the reported asset value was correct; their duty as actuaries was to find the right value of the liabilities. Redington's insight was that, as every insurance or pension liability is merely a stream of cash flows which can be regarded as the negative of asset cash flows, one should use the same interest rate, i, to discount the asset and liability cash flows to come up with their respective values. His immunization theory follows immediately from this idea that there should be equal and parallel treatment in the valuation of assets and liabilities.

If one is convinced that (3.3) is the proper way to value the surplus of a block of business, the strategy for insulating the surplus against interest rate fluctuations merely becomes a consequence of "an elementary piece of differential calculus" (Redington, 1982, p. 85). It follows from Taylor's expansion theorem that the approximation formula

$$S(i + \Delta i) \;\approx\; S(i) + S'(i)\Delta i \tag{3.4}$$

holds for small Δi. Thus by structuring assets and liabilities in such a way that

$$S'(i) \;=\; 0, \tag{3.5}$$

one would have

$$S(i + \Delta i) \;\approx\; S(i),$$

i.e., the surplus remains nearly the same or is "immunized" with respect to a small interest rate change. If the cash flows are not functions of interest rates, then condition (3.5) is equivalent to

$$\sum_t \frac{tA_t}{(1 + i)^t} \;=\; \sum_t \frac{tL_t}{(1 + i)^t}, \tag{3.6}$$

which says that the discounted asset and liability cash-flow streams have the same first moment. Formula (3.6) is the essence of Redington's immunization strategy.

An obvious deficiency in Redington's model is that it allows arbitrage opportunities (free lunches). Taking one more term in Taylor's expansion yields the approximation formula

$$S(i + \Delta i) \;\approx\; S(i) + S'(i)\Delta i + \frac{1}{2}S''(i)(\Delta i)^2. \tag{3.7}$$

Therefore, structuring assets and liabilities such that condition (3.5) and

$$S''(i) \;>\; 0$$

hold would mean, for small $|\Delta i|$,

$$S(i + \Delta i) \; > \; S(i),$$

which implies that, as the interest rate changes, the surplus automatically increases. This automatic "free lunch" in the model arises from using the same interest rate i to discount cash flows of all terms, i.e., there is no distinction between short-term and long-term interest rates and the yield curves are always assumed to be flat.

A remedy for this problem is to replace the discount factor $(1 + i)^{-t}$ in (3.1) and (3.2) with

$$(1 + i_t)^{-t},$$

where i_t denotes the t-period *spot rate* of interest. Formula (3.6) then becomes

$$\sum_t \frac{tA_t}{(1 + i_t)^t} \; = \; \sum_t \frac{tL_t}{(1 + i_t)^t}, \tag{3.8}$$

which is the immunization condition for small parallel yield-curve shifts. We remark that conditions for immunizing a portfolio against larger classes of yield curve shifts can be found in the papers by Fong and Vasicek (1983, 1984), Shiu (1988, 1990), Montrucchio and Peccati (1991), Reitano (1991a, 1991b) and Ho (1992b).

4. Arbitrage Valuation Theory

In deriving the immunization condition (3.6) or (3.8), we have to make the assumption that the asset and liability cash flows, $\{A_t\}$ and $\{L_t\}$, are fixed and certain. This condition certainly does not hold for assets such as callable bonds, mortgage-backed securities (MBS) and interest rate futures, and liabilities such as single premium deferred annuities (SPDA), single premium whole life insurance (SPWL) and universal life insurance (UL). However, Redington's principle of equal and parallel treatment in the valuation of assets and liabilities should still apply. What we need is a more sophisticated method for valuing interest-sensitive cash flows.

The option-pricing theory of Fischer Black and Myron Scholes (1973) has been described as the most important single advance in the theory of financial economics in the 1970's. These authors derived a formula for valuing a European call option on a non-dividend paying stock by showing that the option and stock could be combined linearly to form a riskless hedge, which, by the *principle of no arbitrage,* must earn interest exactly at the risk-free rate. The theory for pricing stock options has been generalized and extended to include the pricing of debt options. In general, a debt security can be viewed as a risk-free asset plus or minus various contingent claims, which usually can be modeled as options. The option-pricing methodology can be applied to value interest-sensitive cash flows.

To fix ideas, let us describe a general set up of a finite-state discrete-time security market model. We assume that the market is frictionless and trades occur only at the times t = 0, 1, 2, ... Let i(t) denote the one-period risk-free interest rate at time t, i.e., if one invests \$1 at time t, one will receive \$[1 + i(t)] at time t + 1. We also assume that there is a finite number of primitive securities. Let $V_j(t)$ denote the value of the j-th primitive security at time t and let $D_j(t)$ denote the dividend or interest payment for the j-th security at time t. (We assume that $V_j(t)$ is the value of the security after $D_j(t)$ has been paid.) Note that, as seen from time s, s < t, i(t), $V_j(t)$ and $D_j(t)$ are random variables. It can be shown that the assumption of no arbitrage is *equivalent* to the existence of a probability measure under which the conditional expectation

$$E_t[V_j(t + 1) + D_j(t + 1)]$$

equals [1 + i(t)]$V_j(t)$, t = 0, 1, 2, ... , and j = 1, 2, 3, ... , i.e.,

$$V_j(t) \;=\; E_t\left\{\frac{1}{1 + i(t)}[V_j(t + 1) + D_j(t + 1)]\right\}. \qquad (4.1)$$

The subscript t following the expectation operator E signifies that the expectation is taken with the knowledge of all information up to time t. In particular, the one-period interest rate i(t) is a constant with respect to E_t (at time t, i(t) is known and not a random variable). The probability measure, normally not the same as the actual probability measure, is called a *risk-neutral* probability measure. That, in a discrete-time model, the absence of arbitrage is equivalent to the existence of a consistent positive linear pricing rule is called (the first half of) the *Fundamental Theorem of Asset Pricing* by Dybvig and Ross (1987). Positive linear pricing rules have appeared in the actuarial literature in the context of equilibrium reinsurance markets [Borch (1960, 1990), Bühlmann (1980, 1984), Sonderman (1991)]. It follows from (4.1) that, for each j and n,

$$V_j(0) = E \left\{ \left[\sum_{t=0}^{n} \frac{D_j(t+1)}{[1+i(0)][1+i(1)] \dots [1+i(t)]} \right] \right.$$

$$\left. + \frac{V_j(n+1)}{[1+i(0)][1+i(1)] \dots [1+i(n)]} \right\}. \qquad (4.2)$$

In general, the value at time 0 of a (stochastic) cash flow stream, {D(t); t = 1, 2, 3, ... }, which can be replicated by the primitive securities, is given by

$$E \left[\sum_{t=0}^{\infty} \frac{D(t+1)}{[1+i(0)][1+i(1)] \dots [1+i(t)]} \right]. \qquad (4.3)$$

See Dalang, Morton and Willinger (1990, Theorem 3.3), Dothan (1990, Section 3.5), Duffie (1992, Part I), Harrison and Kreps (1979), and Huang and Litzenberger (1988, Chapter 8) for technical details. See also Delbaen and Haezendonck (1989).

It should be noted that the expectation

$$E \left[\frac{1}{[1+i(0)][1+i(1)] \dots [1+i(n-1)]} \right]$$

gives the price, at time 0, of an n-period default-free zero-coupon bond. In terms of the spot rate notation in the last section, this value is equal to

$$(1+i_n)^{-n}.$$

The spot rates $\{i_n\}$ are derived from the current prices of noncallable government Treasury bonds and are variables exogenous to the model. Let $V(\{i_n\})$ denote the expected value (4.3). Applying the method of differential calculus or finite differences to V as a function of the initial spot rates $\{i_n\}$ (or other factors), we can derive various price-sensitivity measures, based upon which we can design strategies to manage the assets and liabilities. For example, suppose that we wish to study how

V varies with respect to a parallel shift of the initial yield curve. For a fixed small value h, we calculate the first- and second-order differences

$$\Phi \;=\; V(\{i_n + h\}) - V(\{i_n\})$$

and

$$\Psi \;=\; V(\{i_n + h\}) - 2V(\{i_n\}) + V(\{i_n - h\}),$$

and then apply the approximation formula

$$V(\{i_n + \epsilon\}) \;\approx\; V(\{i_n\}) + \frac{\epsilon}{h}\Phi + \frac{1}{2}\frac{\epsilon}{h}\left(\frac{\epsilon}{h} - 1\right)\Psi.$$

The quantities $-\Phi/[hV(\{i_n\})]$ and $\Psi/[h^2 V(\{i_n\})]$ may be called generalized (or option- adjusted) duration and convexity, respectively. To insulate the surplus of a block of business against small parallel yield-curve shifts, one would match the Φ of the assets to that of the liabilities and try to make the Ψ of the assets larger than that of the liabilities.

To get a better understanding of (4.3), we rewrite it as

$$\sum_{all\ \omega} Pr(\omega)\left[\sum_{t=0}^{\infty} \frac{D(t+1,\omega)}{[1+i(0)][1+i(1,\omega)] \ldots [1+i(t,\omega)]}\right]. \qquad (4.4)$$

Here, each event ω can be identified as an interest-rate path or scenario path; $\{i(0), i(1, \omega), i(2, \omega), \ldots \}$ and $\{D(1, \omega), D(2, \omega), D(3, \omega), \ldots \}$ are the one-period interest rates and cash flows along the path ω. We note that (4.3) and (4.4), in different notation, can be found in Tilley (1988). See also Duffie (1992, p. 23, p. 64).

To apply formula (4.4) we need to specify the risk-neutral probability measure and the one-period risk-free interest-rate process; the probability measure and the one-period interest rates should be such that the model can reproduce an exogenously prescribed set of initial spot rates $\{i_n\}$, i.e., the condition

$$\frac{1}{(1+i_n)^n} = \sum_{all\ \omega} Pr(\omega)\left[\frac{1}{[1+i(0)][1+i(1,\omega)] \ldots [1+i(n-1,\omega)]}\right]$$

holds for all n. The model is usually implemented as a binomial lattice. A simple way for constructing a binomial lattice with an exogenously prescribed initial yield curve is the method of Ho and Lee (1986) or its generalization given by Pedersen, Shiu and Thorlacius (1989). Another efficient method is the technique of forward induction as explained in Jamshidian (1991). The lognormal binomial lattice described in Black, Derman and Toy (1990) is quite popular; also see Black and Karasinski (1991). We remark that Tilley (1992) has criticized the binomial lattices and presented a different method for modeling the evolution of interest rates.

We note that, in practice, it may not be easy to apply formula (4.4) to value a stream of path-dependent cash flows. For example, to value an MBS pool, one would probably need 360 time-periods, each time-period corresponding to one month. In such a model, there are 2^{360} paths. As the mortgage prepayment rate is usually modeled as a function of interest rate history, the method of backward induction cannot be applied. Thus one needs to estimate (4.4) by means of simulation, i.e., one picks a subset Ω' of all paths and calculates

$$\frac{1}{\sum_{\omega \in \Omega'} Pr(\omega)} \sum_{\omega \in \Omega'} Pr(\omega) \left[\sum_{t=0}^{\infty} \frac{D(t+1,\omega)}{[1+i(0)][1+i(1,\omega)] \dots [1+i(t,\omega)]} \right]. \quad (4.5)$$

A systematic procedure for selecting a subset of interest rate paths can be found in Ho (1992a).

Many investment banking firms on Wall Street have constructed valuation models similar to the one described here. See Tilley, Noris, Buff and Lord (1985), Noris and Epstein (1989) and Griffin (1990) for an analysis on SPDA. For applications to MBS, see Jacob, Lord and Tilley (1987) and Richard (1991).

5. Conclusion

Dr. James A. Tilley, physicist, actuary and investment banker, stated in his address to the 23rd International Congress of Actuaries (1988) "that understanding the asset allocation question should begin with an analysis of the market value of the relevant liabilities, and that the market value of the liabilities may best be represented by the theoretical value of the underlying cash flow obligations." Redington, if he were alive, would most certainly agree with this statement.

Except for reinsurance, there is really no market for the exchange of insurance liabilities. It is difficult to actually come up with the *market value* of each liability. However, by constructing an arbitrage-free valuation model such as the one described in the last section, one can compute *relative* market values and price-sensitivity indexes for both assets and liabilities. Based on such information, one can design appropriate strategies for managing assets and liabilities. Indeed, without such a model, it would be hard even to estimate the values of the various options in the assets and liabilities.

It is relatively straightforward to construct arbitrage-free binomial lattices. However, some might complain that it could be very difficult to project the cash flows for certain assets or liabilities. To answer this objection, let us quote Redington (1982, p. 548): "Absolute bedrock is to me the net difference between the income and the outgo A_t - L_t. The actuary who does not know the shape of this cash flow does not know his own company."

REFERENCES

Bierwag, G.O. (1987). *Duration Analysis: Managing Interest Rate Risk.* Ballinger, Cambridge, Mass.

Bierwag, G.O., G.G. Kaufman and A.L. Toevs (1982). "Single-Factor Duration Models in a Discrete General Equilibrium Framework," *Journal of Finance* 37, 325-338. Reprinted in Kaufman, Bierwag and Toevs (1983), 307-323.

Black, F., E. Derman and W. Toy (1990). "A One-Factor Model of Interest Rates and Its Applications to Treasury Bond Options," *Financial Analysts Journal* (January-February), 33-39.

Black, F., and P. Karasinski (1991). "Bond and Option Pricing When Short Rates Are Lognormal," *Financial Analysts Journal* (July-August), 52-59.

Black, F., and M. Scholes (1973). "The Pricing of Options and Corporate Liabilities," *Journal of Political Economy* 81, 637-659.

Borch, K. (1960). "The Safety Loading of Reinsurance Premiums," *Skandinavisk Aktuarietidskrift*, 163-184. Reprinted in Borch (1990), 61-81.

Borch, K. (1990). *Economics of Insurance.* Elsevier, Amsterdam.

Bühlmann, H. (1980). "An Economic Premium Principle," *ASTIN Bulletin* 11, 52-60.

Bühlmann, H. (1984). "The General Economic Premium Principle," *ASTIN Bulletin* 14, 13-21.

Dalang, R.C., A. Morton and W. Willinger (1990). "Equivalent Martingale Measures and No-Arbitrage in Stochastic Securities Market Models," *Stochastics and Stochastic Reports* 29, 185-201.

Delbaen, F., and J. Haezendonck (1989). "A Martingale Approach to Premium Calculation Principles in an Arbitrage Free Market," *Insurance: Mathematics and Economics* 8, 269-277.

Dothan, M.U. (1990). *Prices in Financial Markets.* Oxford University Press, New York.

Duffie, D. (1992). *Dynamic Asset Pricing Theory.* Princeton University Press, Princeton.

Dybvig, P.H., and S.A. Ross (1987). "Arbitrage." In *The New Palgrave: A Dictionary of Economics*, Vol 1, edited by J. Eatwell, M. Milgate and P. Newman, Macmillan, London, 100-106. Reprinted in *The New Palgrave: Finance*, edited by J. Eatwell, M. Milgate and P. Newman, W.W. Norton, New York (1989), 57-71.

Fisher, L. (1980). "Evolution of the Immunization Concept." In Leibowitz

(1980), 21-26.

Fong, H. G., and O. Vasicek (1983). "Return Maximization for Immunized Portfolio." In Kaufman, Bierwag and Toevs (1983), 227-238.

Fong, H. G., and O. Vasicek (1984). "A Risk Minimizing Strategy for Portfolio Immunization," *Journal of Finance* 39, 1541-1546.

Granito, M.R. (1984). *Bond Portfolio Immunization*. Lexington Books, Lexington, Mass.

Griffin, M.W. (1990). "An Excess Spread Approach to Nonparticipating Insurance Products," *Transactions of the Society of Actuaries* 42, 231-248; Discussion 249-258.

Harrison, J.M., and D. Kreps (1979). "Martingales and Arbitrage in Multiperiod Securities Markets," *Journal of Economic Theory* 20, 381-408.

Hawawini, G.A. (ed.) (1982). *Bond Duration and Immunization: Early Developments and Recent Contributions*. Garland Publishing, New York.

Hickman, J.C. (1971). "Investment Implications of the Actuarial Design of Life Insurance Products," *Journal of Risk and Insurance* 38, 571-583.

Hicks, J.R. (1939). *Value and Capital*. Clarendon Press, Oxford.

Hiller, R.S., and C. Schaack (1990). "A Classification of Structured Bond Portfolio Modeling Techniques," *Journal of Portfolio Management* (Fall), 37-48.

Ho, T.S.Y. (1992a). "Managing Illiquid Bonds and the Linear Path Space," *Journal of Fixed Income* 2 no. 1, 80-94.

Ho, T.S.Y. (1992b). "Key Rate Durations: Measures of Interest Rate Risks," *Journal of Fixed Income* 2 no. 2, 29-44.

Ho, T.S.Y., and S.-B. Lee (1986). "Term Structure Movements and Pricing Interest Rate Contingent Claims," *Journal of Finance* 41, 1011-1029.

Huang, C.-F., and R.H. Litzenberger (1988). *Foundations for Financial Economics*. Elsevier, New York.

Jacob, D.P., G. Lord and J.A. Tilley (1987). "A Generalized Framework for Pricing Contingent Cash Flows," *Financial Management* 16 no. 3, 5-14.

Jamshidian, F. (1991). "Forward Induction and Construction of Yield Curve Diffusion Models," *Journal of Fixed Income* 1, 62-74.

Kaufman G.G., G.O. Bierwag and A. Toevs (eds.) (1983). *Innovations in Bond Portfolio Management: Duration Analysis and Immunization*. JAI Press Inc., Greenwich, Conn.

Kocherlakota, R., E.S. Rosenbloom and E.S.W. Shiu (1988). "Algorithms for Cash-Flow Matching," *Transactions of the Society of Actuaries* 40,

477-484.

Kocherlakota, R., E.S. Rosenbloom and E.S.W. Shiu (1990). "Cash-Flow Matching and Linear Programming Duality," *Transactions of the Society of Actuaries* 42, 281-293.

Koopmans, K.C. (1942). *The Risk of Interest Fluctuations in Life Insurance Companies.* Penn Mutual Life Insurance Company, Philadelphia.

Leibowitz, M.L. (ed.) (1980). *Pros & Cons of Immunization: Proceedings of a Seminar on the Roles and Limits of Bond Immunization.* Salomon Brothers, New York.

Lidstone, G.J. (1893). "On the Approximate Calculation of the Values of Increasing Annuities and Assurances," *Journal of the Institute of Actuaries* 31, 68-72.

Macaulay, F.R. (1938). *Some Theoretical Problems Suggested by the Movements of Interest Rates, Bond Yields and Stock Prices in the United States since 1856.* National Bureau of Economic Research, New York. Partially reprinted in Leibowitz (1980) and Hawawini (1982).

Mitchell, R.B. (1974). *From Actuarius to Actuary.* Society of Actuaries, Chicago.

Montrucchio, L., and L. Peccati (1991). "A Note on Shiu-Fisher-Weil Immunization Theorem," *Insurance: Mathematics and Economics* 10, 125-131.

Noris, P.D., and S. Epstein (1989). "Finding the Immunizing Investment for Insurance Liabilities: The Case of the SPDA." In *Fixed-Income Portfolio Strategies,* edited by F.J. Fabozzi, Probus, Chicago (1989), Chapter 7, 97-141.

Pedersen, H.W., E.S.W. Shiu and A.E. Thorlacius (1989). "Arbitrage-Free Pricing of Interest-Rate Contingent Claims," *Transactions of the Society of Actuaries* 41, 231-265; Discussion 267-279.

Redington, F.M. (1952). "Review of the Principles of Life-Office Valuations," *Journal of the Institute of Actuaries* 78, 286-315; Discussion 316-340. Reprinted in Leibowitz (1980), Hawawini (1982) and Redington (1986).

Redington, F.M. (1982). "The Phase of Transition-An Historical Essay," *Journal of the Institute of Actuaries* 109, 83-96. Reprinted in Redington (1986), 492-506.

Redington, F.M. (1986). *A Ramble through the Actuarial Countryside: The Collected Papers, Essays & Speeches of Frank Mitchell Redington, MA.* Institute of Actuaries Students' Society, Staple Inn, London.

Reitano, R.R. (1991a). "Multivariate Duration Analysis," *Transactions of the*

Society of Actuaries 43, 335-376; Discussion 377-391.

Reitano, R.R. (1991b). "Multivariate Immunization Theory," *Transactions of the Society of Actuaries* 43, 393-428; Discussion 429-441.

Richard, S. (1991). "Valuation Challenges: Mortgage-Backed Securities and Collateralized Mortgage Obligations." In *Understanding Securitized Investments and Their Use in Portfolio Management,* edited by K.M. Eades, D.R. Harrington and R.S. Harris, Association for Investment Management and Research, Charlottesville, Virginia, 20-29.

Samuelson, P.A. (1945). "The Effect of Interest Rate Increases on the Banking System," *American Economic Review* 35, 16-27.

Shiu, E.S.W. (1988). "Immunization of Multiple Liabilities," *Insurance: Mathematics and Economics* 7, 219-224.

Shiu, E.S.W. (1990). "On Redington's Theory of Immunization," *Insurance: Mathematics and Economics* 9, 171-175.

Society of Actuaries Committee on Life Insurance Company Valuation Principles (1987). *The Valuation Actuary Handbook.* Society of Actuaries, Itasca, Illinois.

Sonderman, D. (1991). "Reinsurance in Arbitrage-Free Markets," *Insurance: Mathematics and Economics* 10, 191-202.

Tilley, J.A. (1988). "The Application of Modern Techniques to the Investment of Insurance and Pension Funds," *Transactions of the 23rd International Congress of Actuaries, Helsinki* R, 301-326.

Tilley, J.A. (1992). "An Actuarial Layman's Guide to Building Stochastic Interest Rate Generators," *Transactions of the Society of Actuaries* 44, to appear.

Tilley, J.A., P.D. Noris, J.J. Buff and G. Lord (1985). Discussion of "Options on Bonds and Applications to Product Pricing," *Transactions of the Society of Actuaries* 37, 134-145.

Vanderhoof, I.T. (1972). "The Interest Rate Assumption and the Maturity Structure of the Assets of a Life Insurance Company," *Transactions of the Society of Actuaries* 24, 157-192; Discussion, 193-205.

Weil, R.L. (1973). "Macaulay's Duration: An Appreciation," *Journal of Business* 46, 589-592.

9 SCOREKEEPING IN THE 1990'S: FINANCIAL ISSUES OF MULTINATIONAL INSURANCE ORGANIZATIONS

Michael Touhy
Managing Director
Tillinghast, a Towers Perrin Company

Andrew Giffin
Principal
Tillinghast, a Towers Perrin Company

Introduction

To identify the primary financial issues considered to be most important by the world's leading multinational insurance organizations, we reviewed the 1990 annual statements of 29 of them. Companies from the U.S., Canada, U.K., Germany, France, Netherlands, Belgium, Italy, Switzerland, Japan and Australia were included. The companies were selected on the basis of their involvement in life and pension insurance markets, but most of them are also major participants in non-life insurance and other financial service markets. The annual reports covered a wide range of issues, but each organization chose particular issues and operating results to highlight. Comments to follow are limited to what can be readily determined from these public documents.

The common theme running through each of the statements is that multinational insurance groups need better means of scorekeeping — for internal management and for public presentation of their activities and results. Demands for improvement come from increased customer sophistication, from more intense competition and from the complexity of multinational operations.

As part of this analysis, we were looking for clues about what the likely future course of multinationals might be. For example:

- Are multinational expanding their scope of operations, and if so, what regions are favored for expansion?
- What are the financial advantages and disadvantages of multinational involvement?
- What are the likely consequences for major insurers in a particular country market if they do not establish multinational operations?
- How do banking and other financial services fit into this picture?
- What does it take to manage multinational operations' finances effectively?

We use these questions to organize the observations of our sample multinationals. The answers help us to define scorekeeping needs and to identify appropriate new scorekeeping approaches.

Multinational Expansion

The annual report comments reflect a striking difference in attitude between those companies domiciled within Continental European Community countries and the others. Apparently, the opportunities and single market imperatives of 1992 are causing these companies to expand within the EC, and in several cases, in other regions as well.

Most U.S. and U.K. companies are making more modest moves to develop foreign markets. Non-EC Europeans are proceeding cautiously, uncertain of what their opportunities will be as continuing non-EC, members as special status affiliates or as new members. The Australians, facing difficult times at home, are holding for now but appear likely to resume expansion when conditions are more favorable. The Japanese continue to study foreign markets but have yet to announce major moves. Some examples will help to illustrate these broad trends and some of the special circumstances involved with particular companies. Related financial issues are suggested with each example.

For Allianz, Germany's leading insurer, 1990 marked the historic reunification of East and West. Take over of 51% of the previously state owned life and non-life companies of East Germany required a major commitment of resources. However, at the same time Allianz acquired the Fireman's Fund group in the U.S.. It was also developing a joint venture in the U.S.S.R. and a new venture with one of the previously state owned companies in Hungary. A newly incorporated company was being established in Japan. Existing operations in the rest of Europe, the Americas, and the Far East were maintained. Although, most of the company's energy is being devoted to Europe, and its role in the emerging single market within the EC, Allianz is continuing to expand its worldwide scope.

Expansion on this scale requires ready access to capital. Allianz had what the Chairman described as "two rights issues on very favorable terms", increasing capital stock and additional paid capital by nearly 60%. Future justification of these investments, and Allianz's strategy "to build up an adequate presence in all the important or promising insurance markets of the world," will depend on the company's ability to manage effectively life, non-life and related businesses in a wide range of markets and market conditions. The company must also demonstrate these achievements in clear financial terms in future annual reports to shareholders.

Generali, the leading Italian insurer, is in a similar expansionist mode. It states: "product and territorial diversification has been the key to Generali's continued expansion and success in remunerating shareholders."

Although Generali expresses interest primarily for development of European markets, it has been expanding its interest in the U.S. and other markets. Capital management and control of an increasingly complex array of business line are continuing concerns.

M. Claude Bebear, the outspoken Chairman of the French AXA group, explained the group's broad international expansion as an imperative for effective management. Insurance "is becoming a global business," says Bebear. "Powerful international groups are emerging." Meeting increasingly demanding customers, managing risks, evaluating complex statistics, and applying emerging technology require professional skills that must cross national boundaries. Insurance managers must "anticipate international trends in their risk segments. They must be equally comfortable working in Europe, America or Asia." AXA has focused its initial attention on Europe and more recently on North

America. Reinsurance operations in Asia are a precursor to expansion in that region as well.

Others that fit the expansion mode include Aegon (Netherlands), AGF (France), Fortis (AMEV/AG) (Netherlands/Belgium), UAP (France) and Nationale Nederlanden (Netherlands). AIG (U.S.) continues to be expansionist although it is constantly adjusting its position in various markets depending on opportunities and performance. For all of them, the primary financial issues are ones of capital acquisition and the management of an increasingly diverse range of business lines and country markets. All of this must be reduced to a reasonably understandable (and attractive) presentation to shareholders, rating agencies, customers, distributors and employees.

There is another broad category of committed multinationals that, due to current problems in their major markets, are less aggressive in their pronouncements. Their financial focus seems to be more in the areas of cost reduction, consolidation of activities, and preservation of their financial base. The need for reliable internal management information and an effective presentation to constituents is even more acute for these companies.

Aetna of the U.S. has suffered reduced net income and asset value losses from U.S. market problems. Its report to shareholders for 1990 focused on the need to restore rate adequacy, to control health care costs, to adjust services to increased self-insurance and to make more effective use of technology and personnel resources. Losses in the U.K. and growing competition among European companies on the Continent have apparently made Aetna wary of European expansion. Existing Far East operations continue to be developed. The short term realities of the U.S. market have made for a cautious approach to any form of a global strategy. At least, reports to shareholders must demonstrate a cautious approach to foreign markets. Prominent financial issues are directed to internal analysis of assets and operational results.

Similarly, following major acquisitions in the U.K. (London Life and Pearl Assurance) the Australian Mutual Provident Society (AMP) expressed a posture of consolidating its current operations. Declining economic conditions in Australia and New Zealand have strongly influenced this view. AMP states: "although further international growth remains a stated long-term objective for AMP, the priority has been to complete the assimilation of both Pearl and London Life, and to capitalise on the added value that could be provided by AMP." Although both of the U.K. operations had encouraging results for the year, economic conditions in the U.K. are not particularly favorable for immediate expansion.

National Mutual, also of Australia, cited similar operating conditions but remains poised for renewed international development. Following government disapproval of its proposed merger with the ANZ banking and insurance group, National Mutual is modifying its purely mutual status to add a share capital component to raise equity capital. The motto "our strength in a global arena," appearing on most of the pages of the annual report, indicates the company's view of its future. Capital acquisition is obviously a key issue. Improving financial controls on operations was also cited.

Prudential (U.K.) reported that "1990 was a difficult and disappointing year for Prudential." However, based on profits from long term business, dividends were increased. Declines in U.K. asset values and investment returns dominated the results. The 1990 results also reflect losses on Prudential's attempts to develop estate agency business in the U.K. Established Canadian and Australian operations continued to produce profit. Prudential's U.S. subsidiary, Jackson National, maintained profitability with continued growth, offsetting asset value reductions. Newer Continental European operations in Italy,Netherlands and Ireland continue to develop with additional expansion on the Continent to come from direct sales from the U.K. New operations in Singapore and Hong Kong are developing gradually. No further expansion plans were announced. Financial concerns related primarily to general economic and market conditions affecting established operations.

Prudential (U.S.) also emphasized stabilization efforts in the financial security conscious U.S. No mention was made of non-North American operations in the Chairman's message. Participation in European and Far Eastern markets was not featured. Metropolitan (U.S.) mentioned developing international operations but its annual report was devoted primarily to issues of financial security, quality and strength.

Nippon Life (1989) and Dai-Ichi both referred to intentions to expand international involvement but no specific moves were identified. Dai-Ichi's near 10% acquisition of interest in Lincoln National is a first step.

Meiji Mutual's report focused primarily on developments in the Japanese market, including the effects of the decline in the stock market and related decline in single premium products. Meiji expanded its participation in the U.S. market through acquisition of Hawaiian Life in

1991, to be merged with the existing Pacific Guardian Life operation. Apart from a 10% interest in a Brazilian company, Meiji, like the other major Japanese companies, has yet to make a major move to become more active in foreign insurance markets. Cited financial issues are primarily involved with domestic market management.

The Swiss companies are in the awkward position of having extensive operations in the EC countries but, as Switzerland is not yet a member of the EC, their opportunities within the EC are not yet clear. For example, Swiss Life highlighted economic and political instability and only limited extensions of existing foreign market involvement. Complications in presentation of results were noted, resulting from the transfer of the U.K. branch operation to a new subsidiary and understatement of business growth due to adverse currency exchange rates. Swiss Life's involvement in markets outside Europe is through its employee benefits network of associated companies in 31 countries.

Winterhur expressed similar concerns, although it announced an acquisition in Austria and assumption of full control of operations in Hong Kong, Singapore and Malaysia, previously shared with Norwich Union. Its current position was summarized as: "whereas there are countries in which we are making concerted efforts to expand, there are markets in which we are purposely exercising restraint for profit reasons." Changes in reporting formats were highlighted to give more "transparency", including more detail on individual country and business line results and new methods of consolidation. More precise measurement and presentation of results was an expressed objective.

These examples suggest that the primary interest in multinational expansion comes from Europe and involves primarily European markets. The key driver appears to be the emerging EC single market where operating conditions will gradually become more uniform across national borders.

Multinational participation suggests some important financial issues that any active player must address. Where will the capital come from to support entry into, and development of, new markets? How will financial performance be measured and reported for each operation and overall? How will multinationals determine when to enter, exit, expand or contract in any particular market?

Financial Advantages and Disadvantages of Multinational Operations

What do the multinational have to say about the value or importance of globalization? The wide range of current positions and apparent attitudes about multinational participation provides a very confusing picture of whether there is any global imperative for major insurers.

If the necessary capital can be mobilized and if there is a reliable means for making investment choices, how can multinational operations be used to advantage? What are the pitfalls to avoid? We now look at some of the prominent reasons given for adding foreign operations and some of the financial issues associated with them.

Participation in Growth Markets

A major attraction of foreign markets for companies in well developed markets such as the U.S. and U.K. is the opportunity to participate in significantly higher growth rates than are being experienced in domestic markets. High growth areas such as the Far East (e.g., Taiwan, South Korea), Southern Europe (e.g., Italy, Spain) and potentially Central and Eastern Europe (e.g., Poland, Hungary) have attracted considerable attention. But, development of operations in each market requires special infrastructure development efforts and cultural adaption. That generally means either a high cost acquisition and/or deferred profit realization on a long term new company development.

A new entrant requires existing, or access to new, capital, must be able to rationalize profit deferral to shareholders and must be capable of adapting to the new environment.

Diversification of Risks

The contrast between results reported in the annual reports in Continental Europe and North America, the U.K. and Australia are striking, particularly in life insurance. Although financial markets are increasingly linked in terms of general economic conditions, countries vary in insurance market development through such factors as tax, pension legislation and other financial service regulatory changes. In non-life insurance, loss experience, such as the major storm damage that affected results in Northern Europe, varies country to country and line to line.

Multinationals need to be aware, through appropriate financial analysis, of the patterns of risk variance by market to avoid concentration in markets with the same factors and cycles. A good mix of manageable risks can reduce significantly the overall risk profile of the group. However, each line of business must be managed effectively to gain the benefits of risk diversification.

Leverage Competitive Strengths

Similar competitive requirements in multinational markets can provide opportunities for economies of scale in the application of technologies and operating methods. Unfortunately, too many companies merely assume that operating methods, that provide competitive advantage in one market, will have the same effect in others. Each market must be evaluated in its own competitive terms. However, many operating methods can be effectively exported if they are carefully adapted to market differences country to country. AXA's rationale for multinational activity is founded on this idea.

One of the most difficult problems for life insurance is the development of efficient distribution systems. World markets have a wide variety of distribution methods and most markets would support more efficient varieties. BAT Industries says "we are determined to improve our distribution capabilities," through involvement in foreign and domestic markets (e.g., Allied Dunbar in Spain, Eagle Star with the Bristol & West Building Society in the U.K. Multiple country experience can provide important insights into how distribution can be improved in each situation. But, the real value of alternative distribution systems can only be determined if their impact on profitability is measured.

In non-life insurance the demand for multinational attention is even greater. Individual risks do not necessarily stay within national boundaries. Exposures are affected by multinational trends. Development of risk evaluation and claims management systems can gain significantly from broad multinational experience. But, as many London market companies have learned in U.S. liability insurance markets, participation in foreign markets requires a good understanding of the prevailing risk trends.

Meet the Needs of Multinational Clients

As an insurer's clientele builds multinational operations or is more active in multinational affairs, insurers have been compelled to provide for multinational insurance needs or lose business to competitors who can. The options include direct foreign operations or international cooperation with insurers in other markets. There are many examples of both approaches, including life and non-life pooling arrangements.

Of course, an insurer must be sure that there is adequate demand to justify foreign entry. Realistic projections of business, and the financial dynamics that go with it, are essential before taking the plunge.

Conclusion

From a financial perspective, involvement in multinational markets can provide new growth opportunities, risk diversification, leverage of competitive strengths and improved customer service. However, managing the various market conditions and differences in operations is complex. For companies unfamiliar with such influences as currency exchange risks on operating results and international tax treatments, or with various cultural differences, apparently favorable opportunities can turn into unexpected nightmares. As with most insurance risks, the opportunities are more likely to be exploited when the effort required is well understood and appropriately "priced", in terms of financial and human resources.

Consequences of Not Participating

Today, there are many important differences in operating conditions among the EC countries. As trade barriers are reduced, participation across border will become easier. Competitive threats for single country operators will increase. Purely domestic players are likely to be forced into smaller and smaller market niches. Thus, for major EC based companies to focus on expansion within the EC is probably necessary. To be considering a broader range of "European" countries from the U.K. to the Baltics is also probably an important consideration for the long term .

In other country markets, the need to be multinational for domestic market success may be more limited. Certainly, companies serving multinational clientele require either multinational operations or affiliations to meet customer needs. But for most U.S., Japanese or other non-Europeans the choice has more to do with comparing domestic opportunities for growth and profitability with opportunities in foreign markets. The value of multinational experience may be significant for improving domestic competitiveness but the cost of acquiring the experience may be more expensive than the benefit. Comments from the annual reports certainly do not yet suggest broad scale multinational imperatives outside Europe.

However, world insurance markets are changing rapidly. The major U.S. companies face a difficult domestic market and limited capital, compared with many foreign companies. These conditions have limited their enthusiasm for expansion in foreign markets. Yet, Americans will face a more difficult competitive environment in Europe if they wait until the EC and other European companies have restructured the market. They are also likely to face greater participation by well capitalized foreign companies within the U.S. markets. If the large European and Japanese companies can manage multinational operations effectively, they could make multinational operations more valuable for domestic market competition

Banks and Insurance

The rapid confluence of banking and insurance services in Europe and many other parts of the world suggest strongly that current barriers to joint marketing of these financial services will be short lived. Separation of underwriting functions may remain but common control of banking and insurance operations also seems inevitable from a world perspective.

Clearly, the majority of major multinationals are positioning themselves for a combined presentation of banking and insurance products. For example, the recent combination of AMEV of the Netherlands and Groupe AG of Belgium (recently renamed, Fortis) includes the AMEV insurance interests, AMEV's VSB Groep banking operations, AG's insurance and banking interests, mutual fund operations, fund management operations and other financial services. The Fortis group is clearly positioning for European expansion in bank and insurance operations, combined.

The French and Spanish life insurance markets are heavily influenced by bank ownership and combined operations. The German and Italian markets have more recently added bank and insurance combinations. In the U.K., where banks and building societies have long been active marketers of mortgage endowments and other products as independent intermediaries, nearly all are becoming exclusive representatives of single companies or forming their own insurance operations.

Even without direct control, cooperative arrangements are actively being pursued (e.g., Allianz and Dresdner Bank in Germany, numerous marketing arrangements in the U.S.) AIG's entry in Hungary is through a joint venture with the Cooperative Savings Bank. Response to need for quick development of distribution in developing markets is likely to come largely through bank related ventures such as this.

Combinations of banking and insurance are already a prominent feature of multinational insurance group activity. Involvement in ventures in banking, even joint marketing ventures, introduces complex new financial management and reporting issues that must be resolved to assure good information about profitability and maintenance of adequate capital by line of business.

Financial Management of Multinationals

Now that we have identified some of the apparent directions of major multinational insurers, and considered some of the implications, what does this suggest about financial management? The previous observations suggest the following financial issues:

- Capital Acquisition and Application
- Managing and Reporting Performance
- Selecting Points of Entry and Exit, Expansion and Contraction
- Economics of Scale and Cost Reduction
- Managing Risk Diversification

We will suggest financial management methods for each of these areas. But first, there is a more basic issue of management information that comes into play with all of these issues. Multinationals face the difficult task of measuring and reporting results of operations that function pursuant to various accounting rules and local market conditions.

Basic Scorekeeping

Insurance companies are required to maintain accounts that vary significantly within each country. Most statutory systems are designed to apply conservative measures of assets and liabilities for public protection.   Reserves are often required at levels well above best estimates of ultimate requirements. Expenses are often recognized early in the life of an insurance contract, deferring profit recognition. Minimum capital requirements vary significantly by country.

These systems tend to distort the apparent profitability of insurance companies, particularly for long term lines of business. For example, in life insurance, many profitable lines show significant losses in early years because of high first year acquisition costs that may not be deferred to match following year revenues. A combination of restricted deferrals of acquisition expenses and conservative reserves tend to delay profit recognition until after policies have been on the books for several years.   The timing of profit recognition can make a company with declining profitability look better in the current year than one building a solid base for increased profitability.

GAAP accounting has been used in the U.S. to reduce the valuation and profit recognition timing problems. Similar methodologies, designed for reporting to shareholders, are being developed in other countries. Several multinationals cited changes in reporting methods to increase recognition of market value of assets and shareholder values in life funds and reserves.

However, these approaches generally suffer from the application of accounting rules not suited to the long term nature of life insurance products. Since acquisition costs are not fully deferred, reported numbers do not reveal low profit business in the year of sale. Further, capital requirements are ignored.

Statutory, GAAP and other modified systems will continued to be required by regulatory authorities, rating agencies, securities authorities and others. Companies will have to consider the implications of business decisions for results under these systems. However, for meaningful measurement of performance, multinationals need more effective scorekeeping methods.

Companies commit themselves to particular profitability patterns through their decisions on the lines of business they write, levels of growth by line and pricing.   The pricing process projects pattern of profits over many years into the future, using a variety of assumptions (e.g., claims, expenses, contract persistency, interest rates). An effective scorekeeping system must do more than capture a calendar year slice of that long term history in the making.

Aegon of the Netherlands has indicated its intention to make better use of embedded value as a management tool. The annual report states: "In our view this tool — which sets a present value on the identifiable future results of the existing portfolio — will provide more insight. As a part of an active investor relations program we will bring this approach to the attention of the investment community."

Embedded and appraisal values are commonly used in the evaluation of companies for purposes of mergers and acquisitions. Embedded value analysis estimates the value of business currently on the books. Appraisal value analysis adds value associated with future business potential (i.e., goodwill) based on currently available infrastructure.

To develop embedded values, a model of the company's is force business in built and projections of future distributable earnings are made, taking account of minimum capital requirements (i.e., required surplus) and using current estimate assumptions. Distributable earnings are after-tax statutory earnings (including investment income on assets matching required surplus), less any required surplus increase. The present value of the distributable earnings, plus the value of any excess capital (i.e., excess over required capital), determines the embedded value.

Company models are validated by comparing model results of past periods with actual results. Overall performance is assessed by determining the growth in embedded value from year to year.

To understand the underlying causes of embedded value changes, the assumptions that go into the embedded value calculations are available for analysis. At the conclusion of each period, analyses of variances in embedded value are performed. Variance analyses identify the source and magnitude of variations in value by line of business.

Thus, in addition to having on overall measure of shareholder value, the primary factors that influence profitability can be identified. When they deviate adversely from profit plans, management knows where operational adjustments are required. Current profit expectations can be included in current pricing. Where actual expense or other pricing allowances do not permit competitive pricing, requirements for operational changes are revealed.

The methodology allows fair comparisons of results by line of business and by country market, subject to varying statutory accounting and solvency margin requirements (public and private). For each line of business statutory surplus, or solvency margin, requirements are determined. Part of the cost of operation is paying for capital employed (i.e., required surplus) in each line. Present value calculations apply discount rates that reflect company assessments of the inherent business risks, and related costs of capital, of each line.

Internal performance measurement is enhanced by identifying product lines, country markets and particular pricing factors with strong and weak performance. Both the central management and the business unit managers have a reliable and consistent basis for evaluating results. Efforts undertaken to correct problems discovered can be described to shareholders in hard times and performance over pricing assumptions can be used to explain the source of higher distributable earnings in good times.

Introduction of embedded value analysis, as suggested by Aegon and others provides a useful view of the development of business, assuming consistent application of the methodology over time. Some have criticized the methodology as dependent on assumptions of future events. Yet, current reserves, pricing and many other bases of day-to-day operations require decisions based on the same assumptions. Embedded value analysis strengthens these activities by continually reevaluating those decisions on the basis of experience as it accumulates.

Capital Acquisition and Application

Allianz recently made rights issues to support its expansion efforts. Success in these efforts require some luck in having good investment market conditions for an offering and an attractive investment story to tell. The latter depends on consistently sound management and presentation of reliable financial information.

Mutual organizations have special problems acquiring new capital because of their organizational structure. This can be avoided by raising capital through a down stream holding company, by demutualizing or, as National Mutual is doing, by adding a stock company component to the capital structure.

BAT Industries reported rationalization of its holdings to emphasize tobacco and financial services, improving its ability to support expansion from internal resources. Opening of new free market economies are expected to provide growth markets for tobacco, with favorable cash flow characteristics. The company expects to be able to increase investment in financial services.

Whether capital is to be acquired from public markets or from internal resources, the value of its deployment within particular business lines and markets must be justified. The discount rates used in embedded value analysis reflect cost of capital within the group, including the variation in business risks within each business line and market. In addition to determing the level of capital required for each business line, company value analysis helps to isolate value added or subtracted by new sales. Value analysis facilitates capital allocation decisions.

Managing and Reporting Performance

Many of the companies in the survey reported attempts to reconcile different accounting treatment of insurance business results from country to country. Legal & General of the U.K. described efforts within the company and in the Association of British Insurers to provide more realistic presentations of life insurance profitability, including shareholder values retained in the life fund and earlier recognition of profit.

As described above, these methodologies generally result in some improvements but are still not consistent with company pricing and appraisal approaches. However, statutory and modified forms of accounting are important, as they determine, respectively, solvency and shareholder reported earnings.

No reporting system will correct inherent weakness in profit generating potential. The greatest value of the embedded value method is its exposure of the performance of profit generating characteristics compared with pricing and planning assumptions. If acquisition or maintenance expenses exceed pricing allowances, should the method of operation, the pricing assumption, or both be changed? What is to be done about persistency or mortality trends in life insurance, or claim frequency or severity trends in non-life insurance, that are out of line with pricing assumptions? It is not enough to know where the negative variances are. This information, collected on a regular basis, must be used for management action.

For multinationals, this is certainly a complex problem. Yet, if a wide range of business lines are to be operated effectively, in various market settings, each situation must first be understood at this level of detail. Then, organizational structures, monitoring systems and corrective efforts may be directed toward critical profit generating factors.

Selecting Points of Entry and Exit, Expansion and Contraction

The same company modeling methodology can be used to determine the feasibility of new market entries and to determine probable returns to further expansion or contraction of the business. Expected future business can be modeled to reveal future patterns of distributable earnings. Comparisons of prospective new operations and continuation of existing ones can be made on a consistent basis.

Sensitivity analysis of the influence of particular pricing factors (e.g., interest rates, expenses, lapses) on profit results can alert management to those that need to be monitored carefully.

This methodology is well established for appraising the value of an insurance company in the case of acquisition or merger. Too often, this valuable information is not used in the formation of business plans and monitoring of performance in acquired companies post-acquisition. Too often we have completed similar appraisals three of four years after an acquisition only to find significant value lost through misguided business planning. Appraisal analysis can and should be used as the foundation for business plans for an acquired company, to protect and extend the value represented in the purchase price.

Europeans accuse U.S. companies of making their expansion or contraction plans on the basis of quarterly results. To avoid the tendency to over react to short term financial results, financial measurement of results over a period of years is needed. So long as business development remains on plan, expansion efforts should continue. If short term conditions force changes in plans (e.g., unavailability of needed additional capital), at least the consequences (i.e., lost value) can be determined and the losses minimized.

Embedded and appraisal value analysis can help a company explain continuation of new market expansion to shareholders and the local financial community when longer term results appear favorable, even when local market conditions are demanding special caution. Consistent application of these methods will build confidence in management's ability to identify long term opportunities that may not be evident in short term outlooks.

Economies of Scale and Cost Reduction

Even within the EC, where trade barriers will soon make it theoretically possible to sell products of one country in another, direct exportation of products and operating procedures from one country to another will be limited for some time. Yet, sharing of generic operating methods, product concepts and management methods can contribute to the success of operations in various markets, if they are carefully adapted to local market needs.

One example is the financial modeling we have been describing. Consistent methodologies for such things as embedded values have been adapted for local variations in accounting and product designs to provide centralized financial management tools.   Although there are many complex issues to be resolved concerning proper use of the methodology, our experience with multinationals suggests that what is learned about the operating conditions of each unit makes the effort worthwhile.

Many of the multinationals in our survey highlighted efforts to reduce costs. Analysis of the variance in distributable earnings results, from planned levels, that identifies the source of variance by pricing factor and by business line, helps multinationals identify more specific targets for cost reduction. This analysis can help the group make difficult decisions for centralizing or decentralizing functions for the greatest cost effectiveness.   The need to correct a particular problem in a line (e.g., expense levels) can be distinguished from more general problems (e.g., competitive pricing below current costs) that make profitability difficult to maintain for the line overall.

Managing Risk Diversification

How much capital is required to meet regulatory or rating agency requirements? How much capital is required to assure protection of the companies against potential adverse operating results? How can these capital requirements be reduced through diversification of risks? These are questions being asked by the multinational for their own planning and by rating agencies that provide public information about their relative financial strength. Recent events in the U.S. have made capital adequacy a hot topic. The U.S. experience will affect multinationals around the world as they are active in the U.S. market and are subject to U.S. ratings.

Very high levels of capital, though comforting as protection, reduce rates of return for shareholders. Risk based capital requirement analyses are being developed to help companies and insurance authorities strike a reasonable balance between adequate solvency margins and excess capital. Rating agencies are using static formulas (i.e., based on financial statement data as of a particular date) to make rating judgments.

Models developed to provide embedded and appraisal values can be used to help estimate risk based capital requirements more precisely (i.e., dynamically, considering patterns of business activity over time). By modeling extreme operating scenarios (e.g., high losses, low interest rates), companies can determine levels of capital required to withstand adverse operating conditions.

Asset-liability management analysis is another valuable tool for risk evaluation and for financial planning. Stochastic techniques can be used to determine exposure to such risks as asset value loss and disintermediation.

Through a combination of these techniques, capital requirements by business line and for the group overall can be determined. Identification of specific risk factors for asset values, reserve adequacy, pricing adequacy and other factors allows multinational to manage their risk profiles and capital requirements. Managements can identify particular actions (e.g., selling risky assets, adding business lines with covariant risk profiles) that will make more effective use of available capital.

Although rating agencies tend to use relatively simple formulas for determining capital requirements, they are currently searching for more reliable means for making judgements. Companies that can effectively, and consistently, explain the risks they face and their methods for covering them will have an easier time securing favorable ratings. Good information on the groups's risk profile is a sign of strong management, an important factor in ratings.

Conclusion

Whether multinationals face a global imperative or not, managing their financial affairs is becoming increasingly complex. The technology exists to combine and breakdown the factors that drive distributable earnings, returns on investment and capital requirements. Company modeling, embedded and appraisal value analyses, profitability variance analysis, risk based capital analysis, and asset-liability management are currently available tools. Multinational are learning to use these tools more effectively. Through them they can make more efficient use of capital and manage their varied business units more effectively.

Multinationals
International Outlook

Country-Companies	Approach	Management Comment
Germany		
Allianz	Expansion	"...build up an adequate presence in all the important or promising insurance markets of the world...in the United States...Eastern Europe...the fast-growing markets of the Pacific...we are making extensive preparation for the single European market."
Italy		
Generali	Expansion	"...objectives...internationality, innovation and high technical standards...Europe has always been a priority...establishing in Eastern European countries."
Switzerland		
Winterthur	Maintain	"...there are countries where we are making concentrated efforts to expand...there are markets where we are purposefully exercising restraint..."
Zurich	Selective Expansion	"...optimal alignment to market segments and customer target groups...exploiting the new market opportunities (in the EC) development in Eastern Europe...taking over NZI Life (in Australia)."

Switzerland (continued)		
Swiss Life	Maintain	"...Swiss Life is in an excellent position to assist clients in meeting challenges of 1992 and beyond."
Netherlands		
Fortis (AMEV/AG) (VSB (Bank) Groep)	Expanding	"...future growth and expansion of their international activities...a leading provider of a wide range of financial services..."
Nationale Nederlanden	Expanding	"...aims to secure a prominent position in the European market...achieve its growth through acquisition of or cooperation with institutions...(a) substantial expansive force in Europe and the rest of the world."
AEGON	Expanding	"...reinforced its international position and will continue its strategy of further expansion. In the United States...we continue to look for suitable acquisition candidates...we see good prospects for the growing insurance market in Southern Europe."

France		
UAP	Selective Expansion	"...the number two insurance group in Europe...commitment...to a dynamic policy of external growth in preparation for the single European market."
AXA	Expanding	"...insurance is...becoming a global business...powerful international groups are emerging...single markets serves as a catalyst...must be equally comfortable working in Europe, Americas or Asia...Plan: Become the leading company in our profession."
AGF	Selective Expansion	"...consolidate our market shares...by 1993 increase premium income (75%)...40% of which through international business...Our Goal: Be one of the five leading European insurers of the year 2000."
United Kingdom		
Prudential	Maintain	"...will in due course be able to sell (our) products in other member states (of the EC) without the necessity of developing an insurance base there...good progress is being made in many territories."
BAT Industries	Selective Expansion	"...vision of financial services as the right growth business...we are increasing the rate of investment..."
Commercial Union	Maintain	"...position the group as a leading European insurer...expansion by organic growth."

United Kingdom (continued)		
Royal	Maintain	"...since 1984 in excess of £500 million of funds have been deployed in purchase of our worldwide life and related financial services operations...a strategic review of our operations to ensure that they are correctly positioned."
Sun Alliance	Maintain	"...has continued to develop its European operations to meet challenges of the single European market...expanding."
Legal & General	Maintain	"...strengthen our position in areas in which we see competitive advantages..."
General Accident	Maintain	"...comprehensive strategic review...of worldwide activities...cancellation of unprofitable...rationalization...restoration."
Japan		
Nippon Life	Looking	"In 1933, Nippon set out to become the world's leading insurance company...maintain and extend its leading role in world financial markets...move further toward becoming an international company."
Dai-Ichi	Looking; Limited Investment	"The world's second largest life insurance company (by in force)...expanding its worldwide network."
Meiji Mutual	Maintain	"Maintain our position as one of the world's leading life insurance companies."

United States		
Prudential	Gradual Expansion	"...big enough to diversify...stay away from some risks that now haunt others."
Metropolitan	Gradual Expansion	"...well positioned to enter international markets...our plan is to move carefully into new markets."
Aetna	Maintain	"...one of the world's leading providers of insurance and financial services...better positioning some businesses to compete...concentrate on improving the results of its more mature operations."
CIGNA	Maintain	"...positioning CIGNA in various key markets...global risk management unit offers comprehensive property-casualty protection...making a significant commitment to direct marketing around the world."
AIG	Continued Expansion and Reposition -ing	"...the leading U.S.-based international insurance organization...entry into...Poland and Hungary...broad geographic diversity...aim to be the most successful insurance organization."

Canada		
ManuLife	Continued Expansion and Reposition-ing	"...Strategically grow and diversify our business...expanding our geographic reach...offset business difficulties in one market with successful growth in others."
Australia		
AMP	Future Expansion	"...international growth remains a stated long term objective...priority has to be assimilation of both Pearl and London Life...tight control of expenditure."
National Mutual	Future Expansion	"...well prepared for the globalization of economies and financial market...our strength in a global area...well placed to take advantage of future economic recovery...we need to have access to additional sources of capital."